In the Doghouse

by Timothy Glass

In the Doghouse
© Copyright Timothy Glass, 2017
All rights reserved. No part of this book may be reproduced, stored or transmitted by any means such as electronic, photocopying, recording or scanning without the written permission from the publisher and the copyright owner.
The distribution of this material by means over the Internet or copying of this book without prior written permission from the publisher is illegal and punishable by law. Platinum Paw Press appreciates your support and respect of the author's rights.
Cover design by Timothy Glass
Illustrations by Timothy Glass
Inside and back cover photo of the Glass Family by Kim Jew

Platinum Paw Press
Visit our website www.platinumpawpress.com

Library of Congress Control Number: 2017938624
ISBN:978-0-9984121-1-5
Printed in the United States of America

Dedication

As always, to my wife, Cathy, my shining star on the darkest night. Thank you for believing in me.

To Charlie Crockett, whose life was cut way too short. Miss you, buddy.

Timothy Glass

Sleepytown Beagles by Timothy Glass

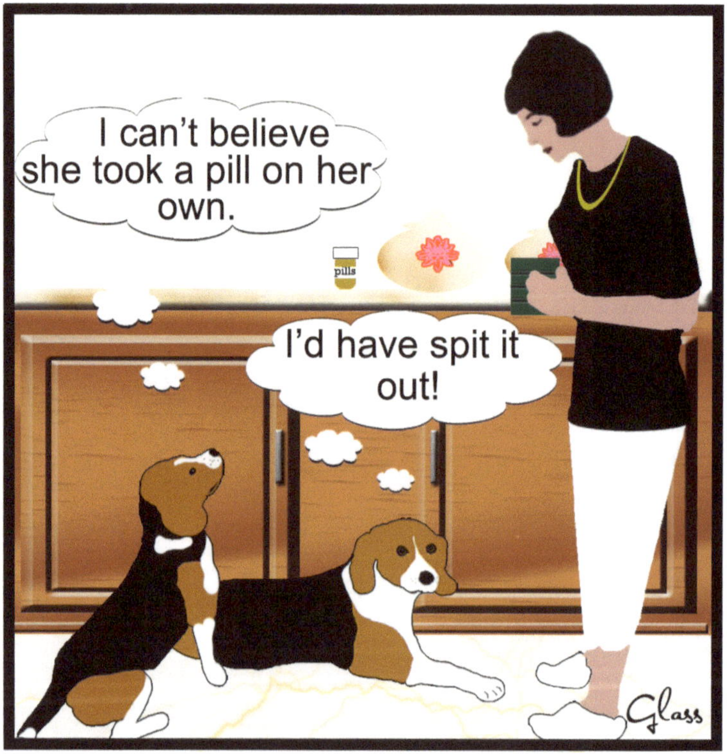
I can't believe she took a pill on her own.
pills
I'd have spit it out!
Glass

Sleepytown Beagles by Timothy Glass

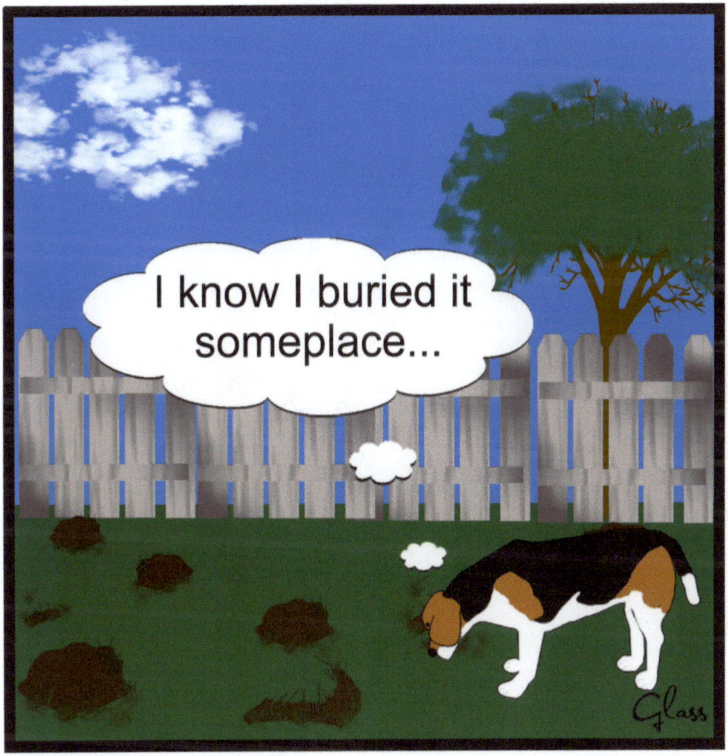
I know I buried it someplace...
Glass

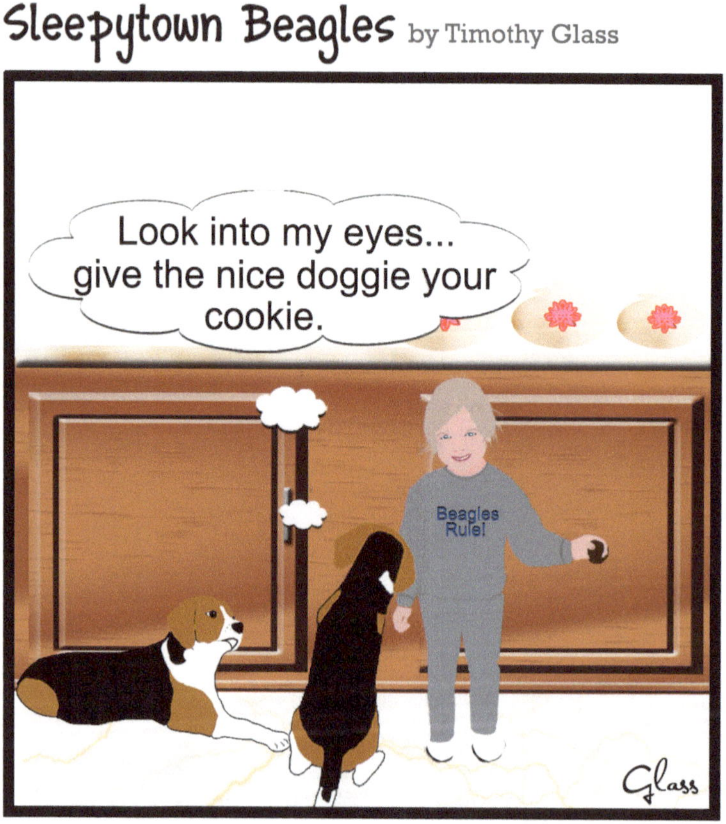
Sleepytown Beagles by Timothy Glass
Look into my eyes... give the nice doggie your cookie.
Beagles Rule!
Glass

Sleepytown Beagles by Timothy Glass

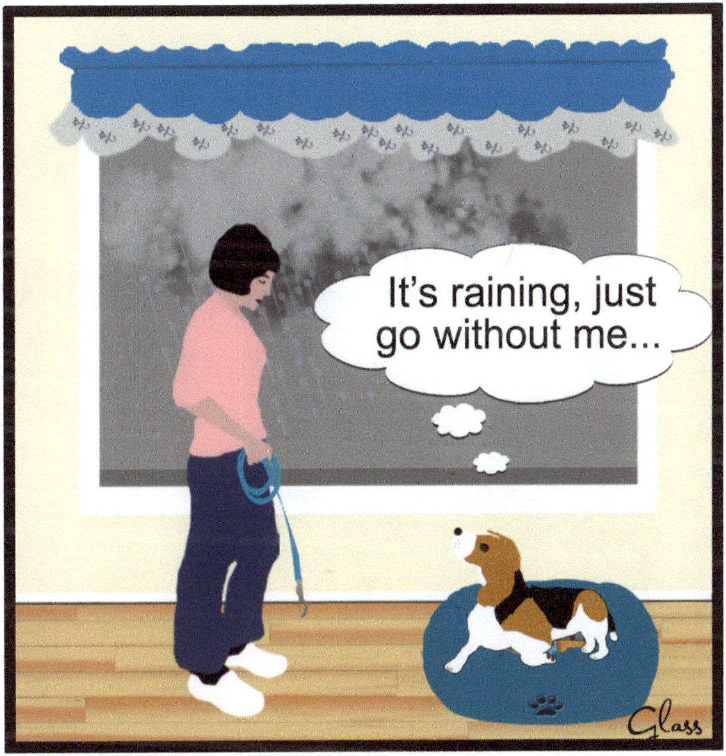
It's raining, just go without me...
Glass

Timothy Glass

Sleepytown Beagles by Timothy Glass

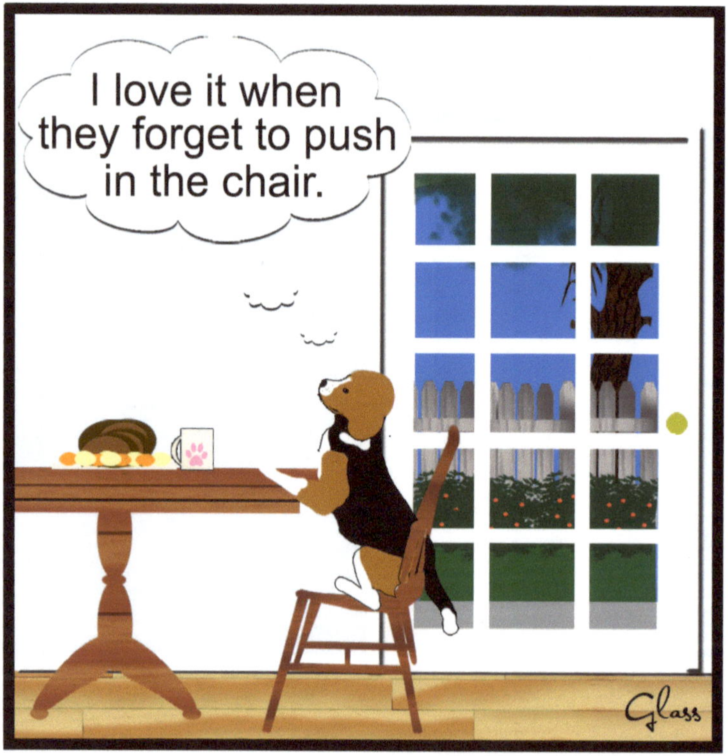
I love it when they forget to push in the chair.
Glass

Sleepytown Beagles by Timothy Glass

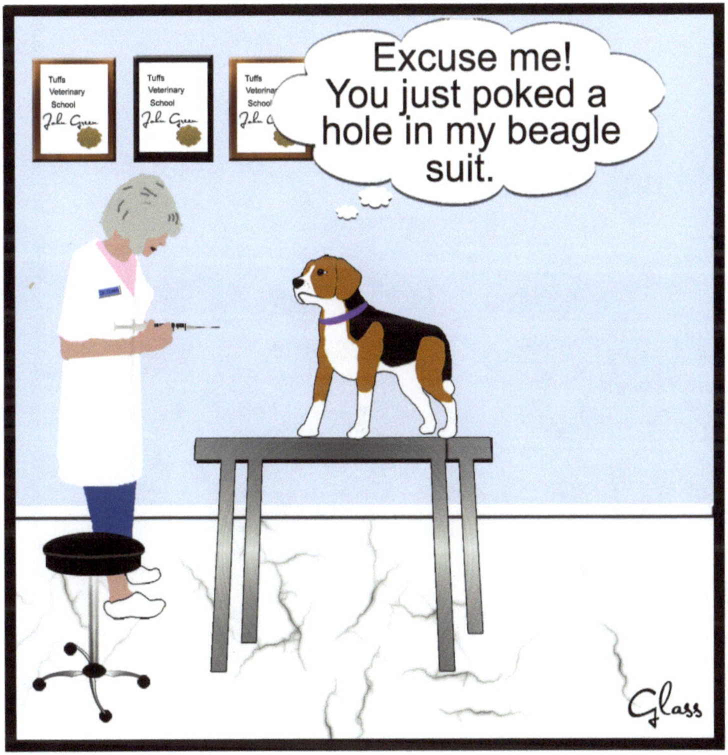
Tuffs Veterinary School
Excuse me! You just poked a hole in my beagle suit.
Glass

Timothy Glass

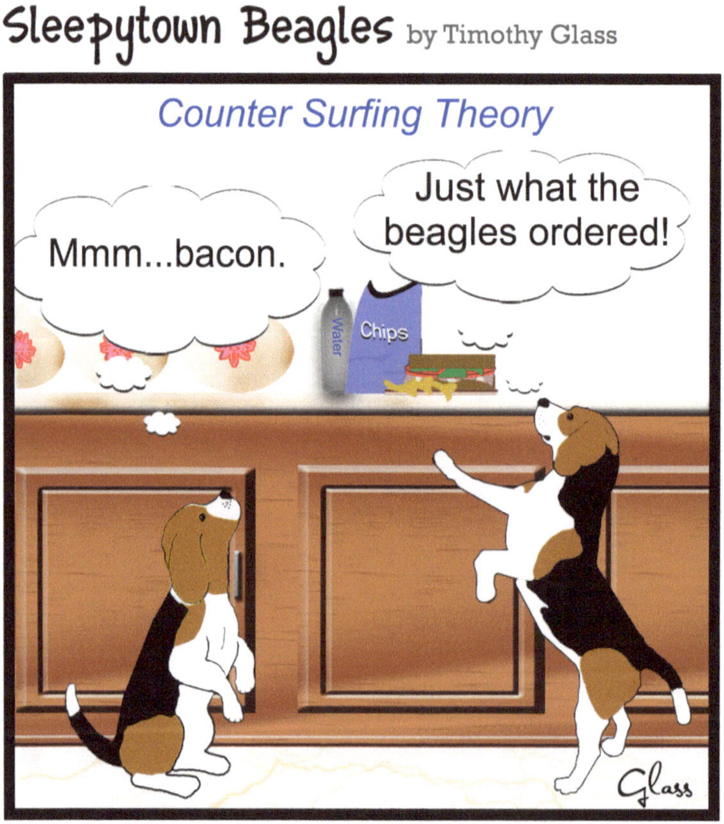
Sleepytown Beagles by Timothy Glass
Counter Surfing Theory
Mmm...bacon.
Just what the beagles ordered!
Water
Chips
Glass

Sleepytown Beagles by Timothy Glass

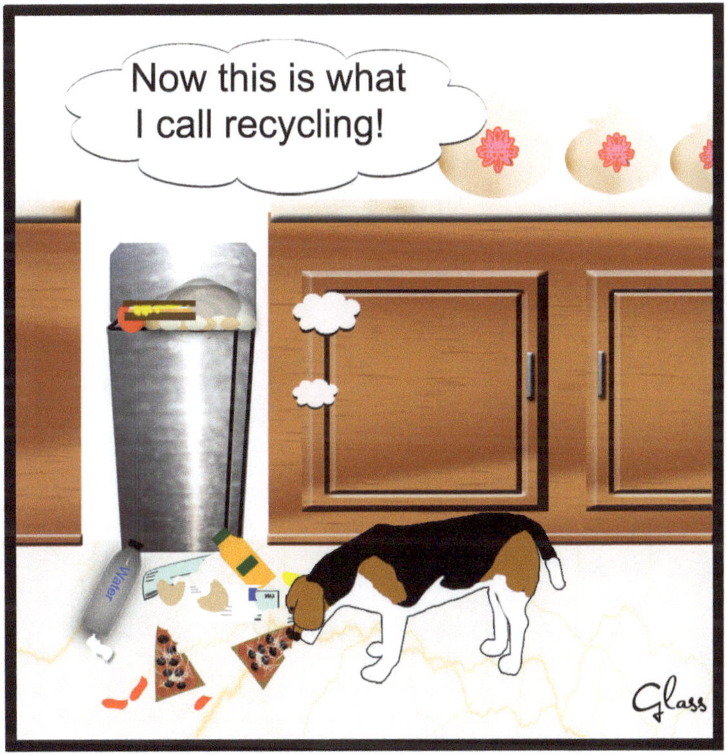
Now this is what
I call recycling!
Water
Glass

Sleepytown Beagles by Timothy Glass

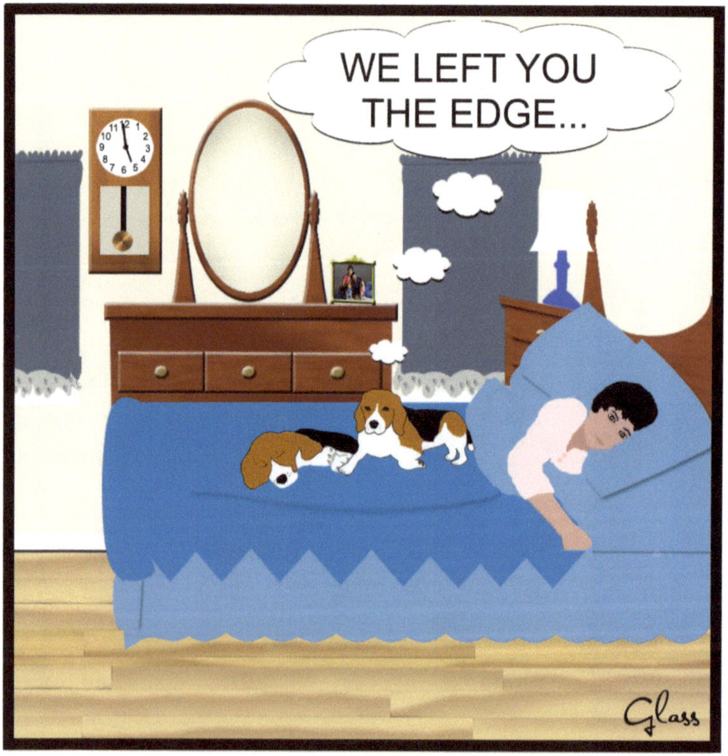
WE LEFT YOU
THE EDGE...
Glass

Sleepytown Beagles by Timothy Glass

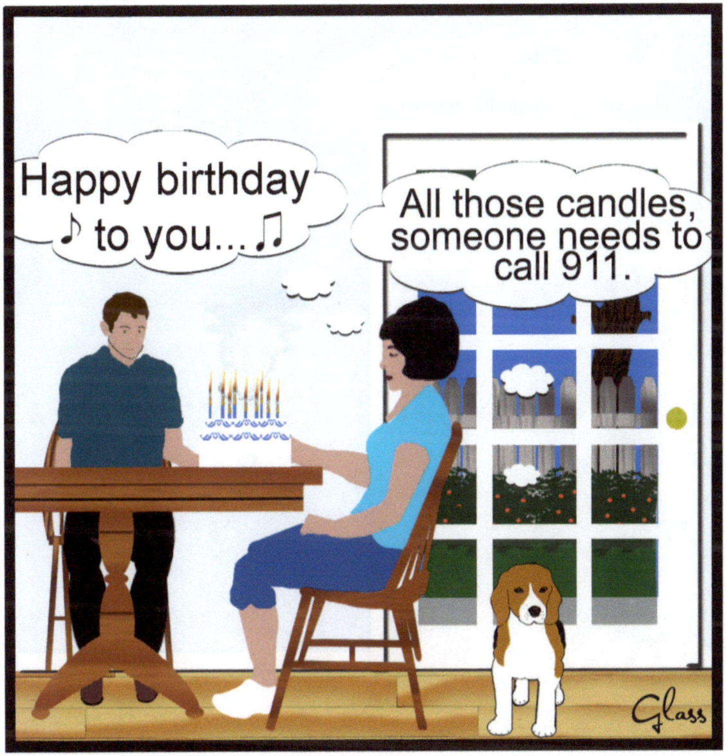
Happy birthday ♪ to you... ♫
All those candles, someone needs to call 911.
Glass

Sleepytown Beagles by Timothy Glass

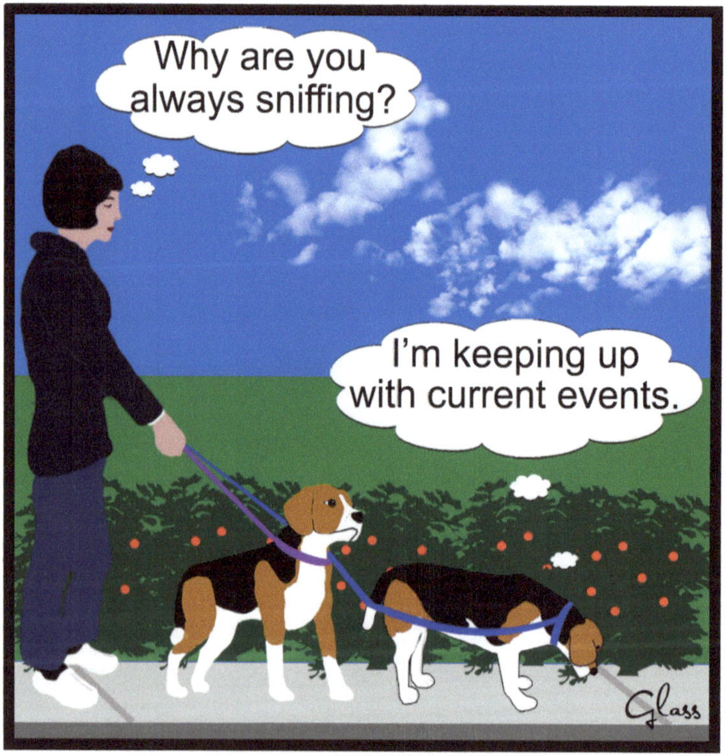
Why are you always sniffing?
I'm keeping up with current events.
Glass

Sleepytown Beagles by Timothy Glass

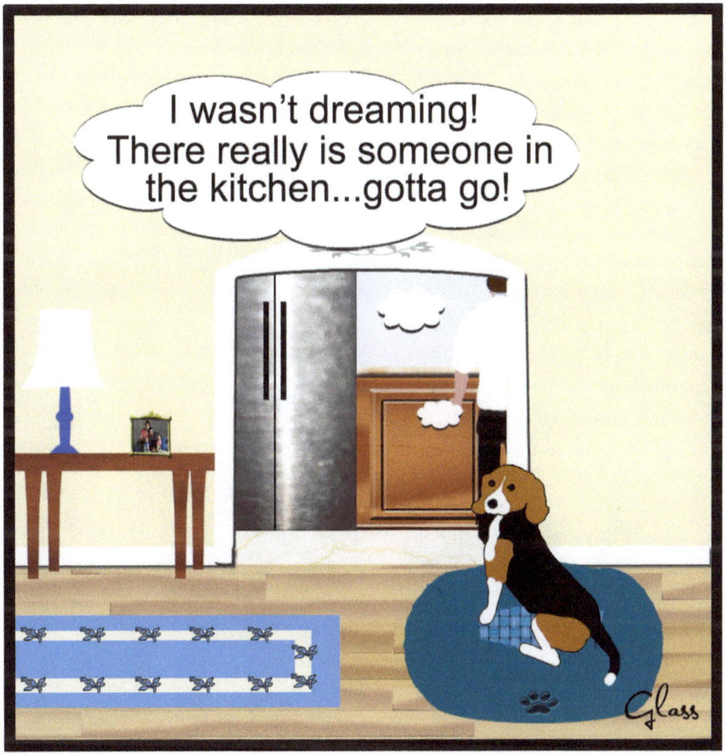
I wasn't dreaming!
There really is someone in the kitchen...gotta go!
Glass

Timothy Glass

Sleepytown Beagles by Timothy Glass

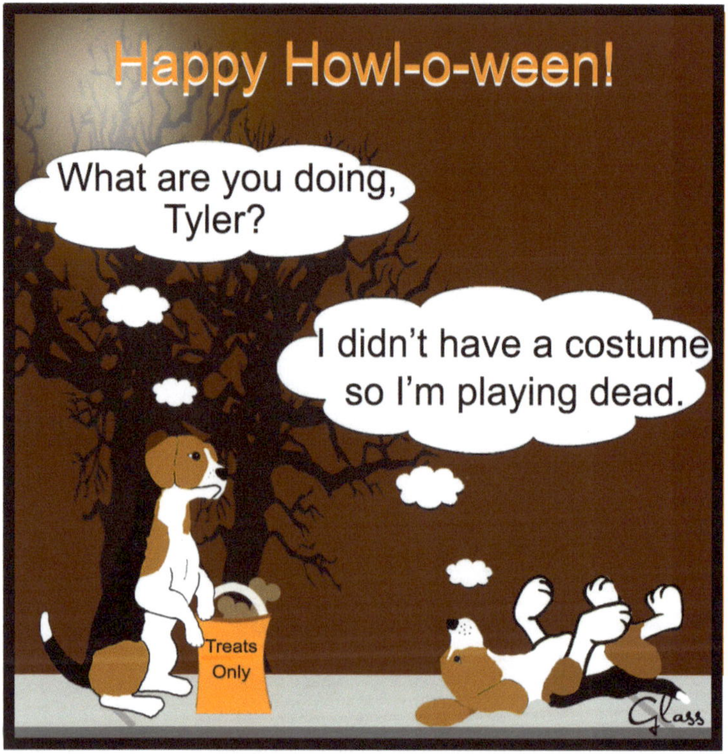
Happy Howl-o-ween!
What are you doing, Tyler?
I didn't have a costume so I'm playing dead.
Treats Only
Glass

Sleepytown Beagles by Timothy Glass

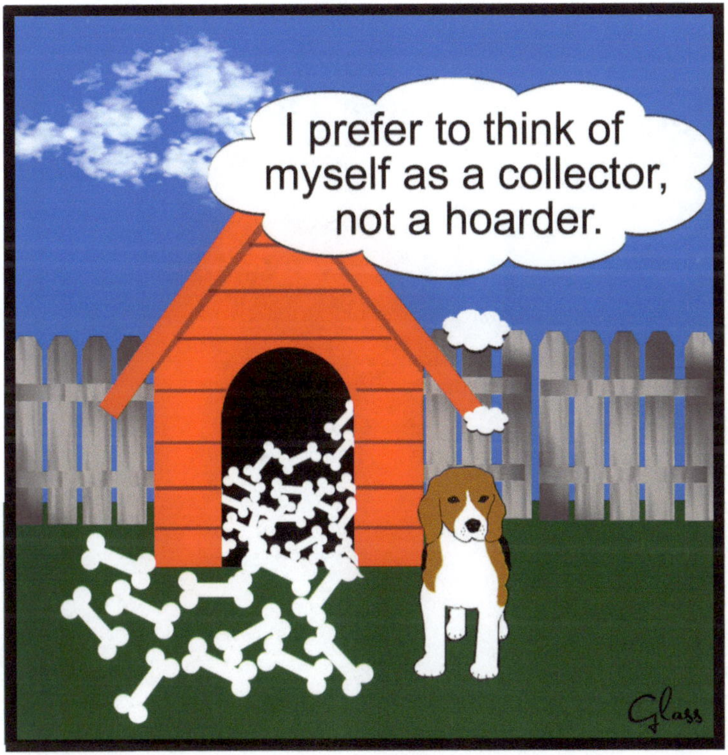
I prefer to think of myself as a collector, not a hoarder.
Glass

Timothy Glass

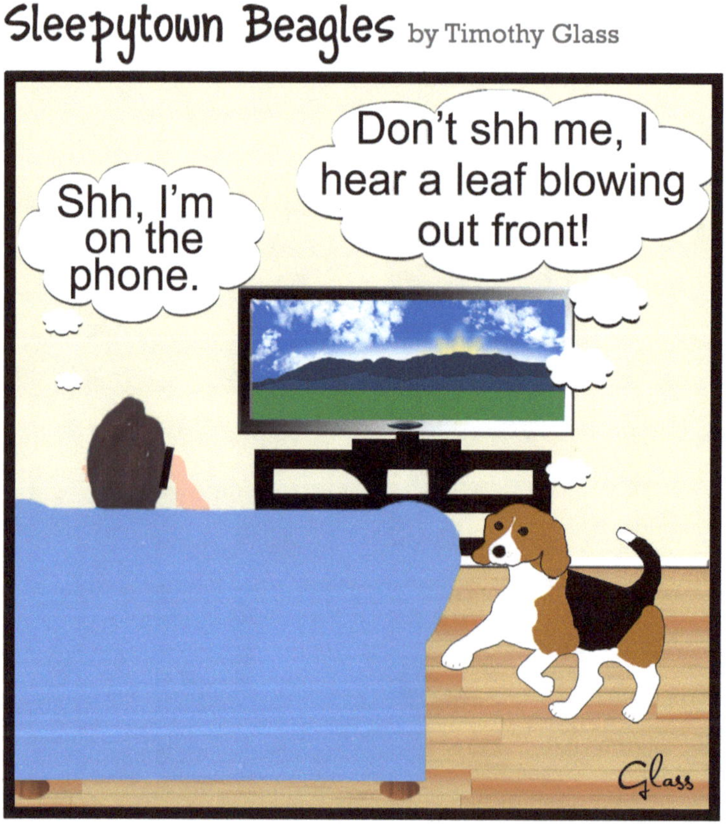
Sleepytown Beagles by Timothy Glass
Shh, I'm on the phone.
Don't shh me, I hear a leaf blowing out front!
Glass

In The Doghouse

Sleepytown Beagles by Timothy Glass

Timothy Glass

Sleepytown Beagles by Timothy Glass

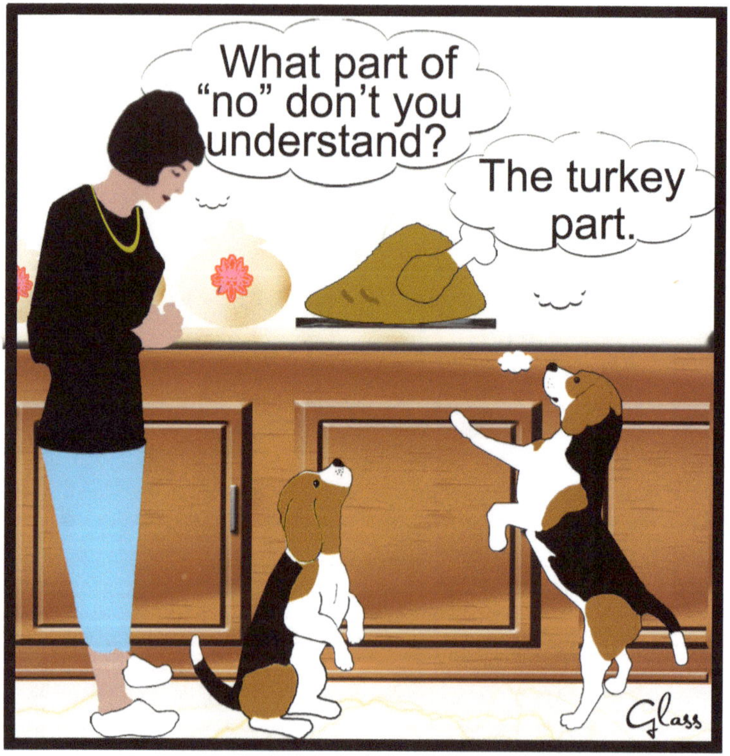
What part of "no" don't you understand?
The turkey part.
Glass

Sleepytown Beagles by Timothy Glass

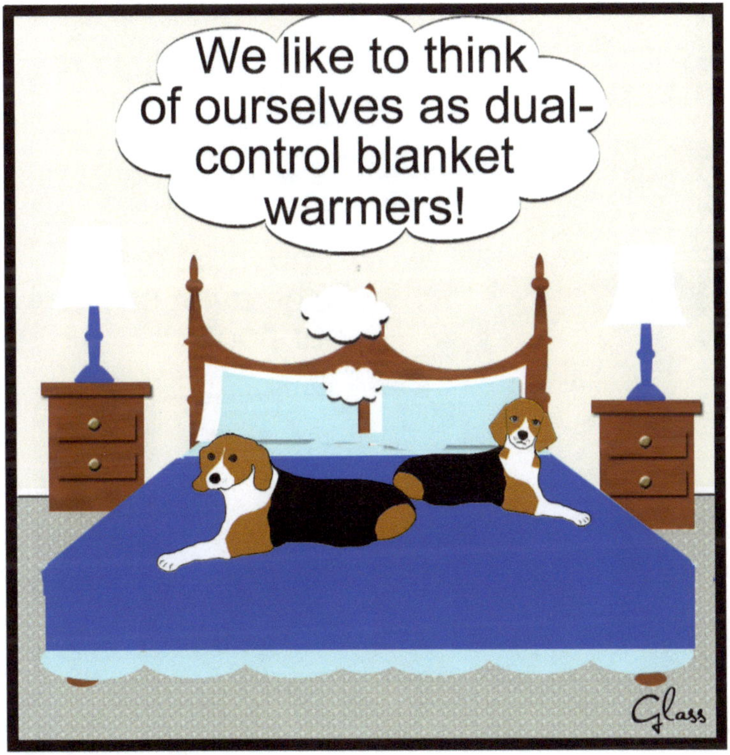
We like to think of ourselves as dual-control blanket warmers!
Glass

Timothy Glass

Sleepytown Beagles by Timothy Glass

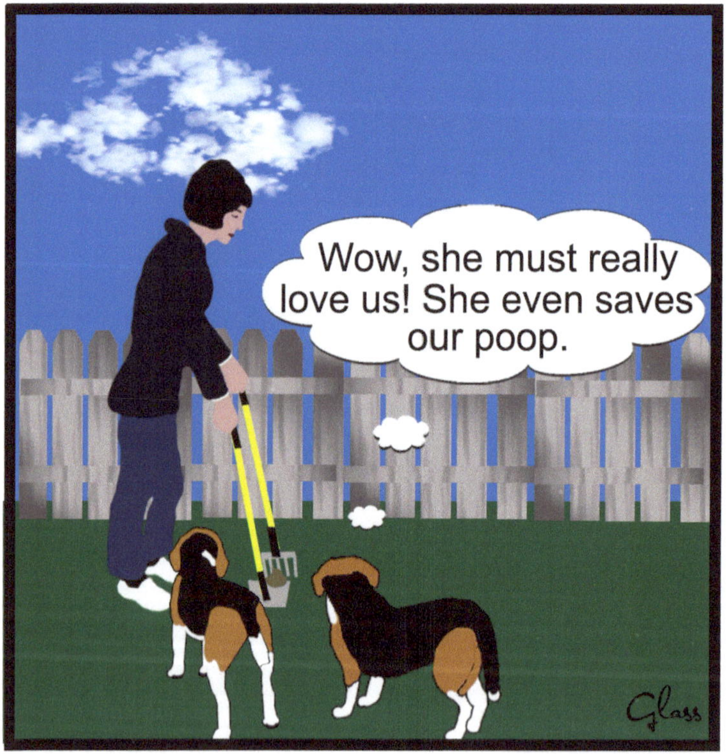
Wow, she must really love us! She even saves our poop.
Glass

Sleepytown Beagles by Timothy Glass

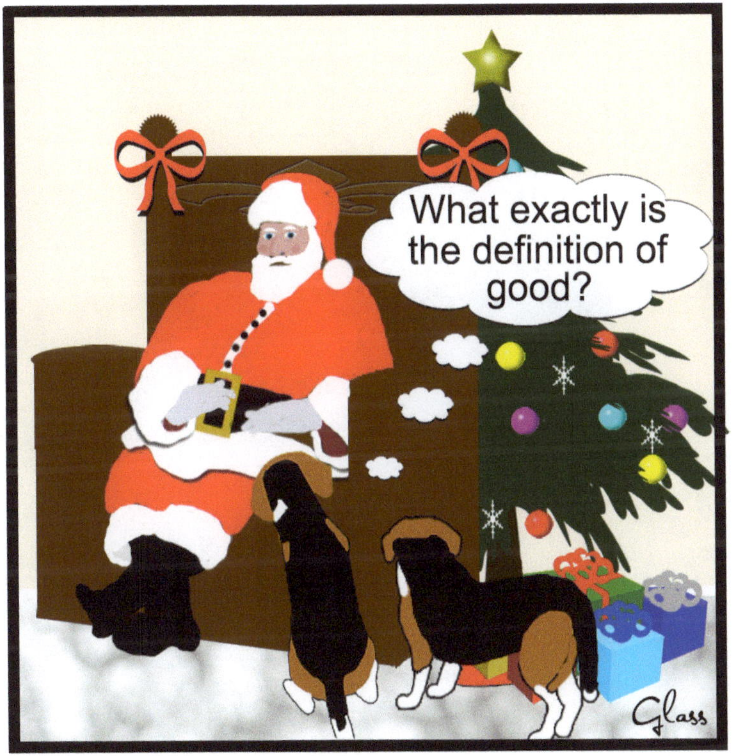
What exactly is the definition of good?
Glass

Timothy Glass

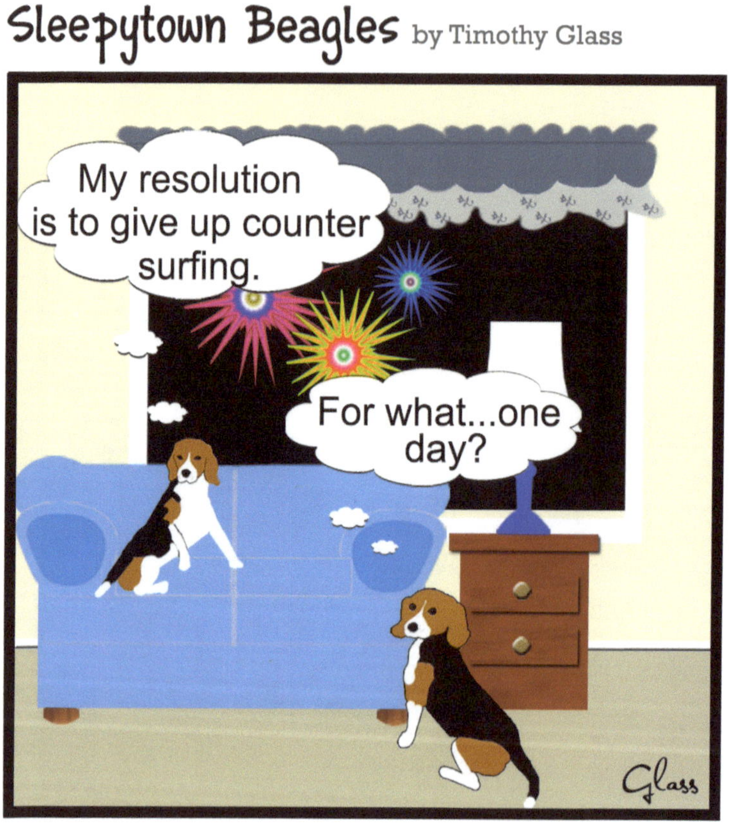
Sleepytown Beagles by Timothy Glass
My resolution is to give up counter surfing.
For what...one day?
Glass

Sleepytown Beagles by Timothy Glass

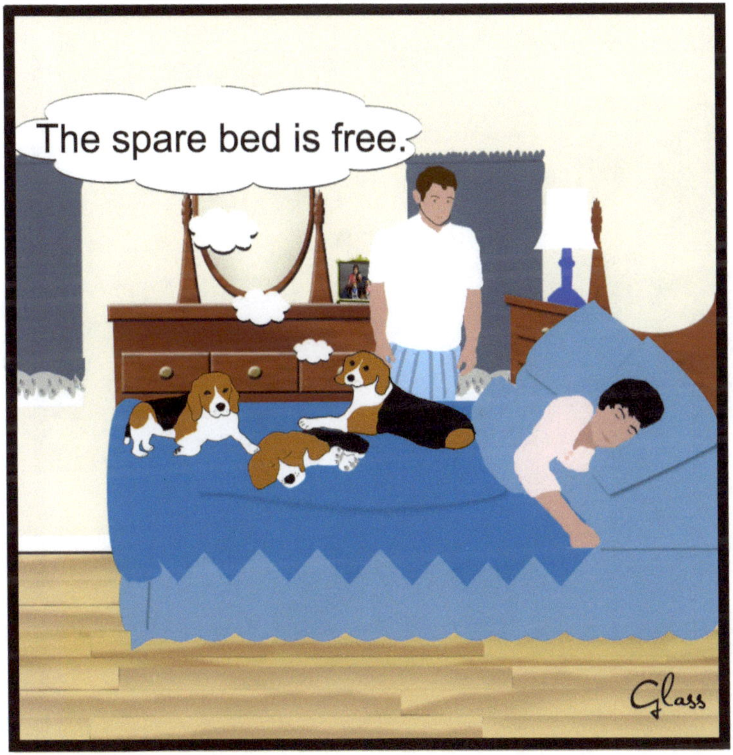
The spare bed is free.
Glass

Timothy Glass

Sleepytown Beagles by Timothy Glass

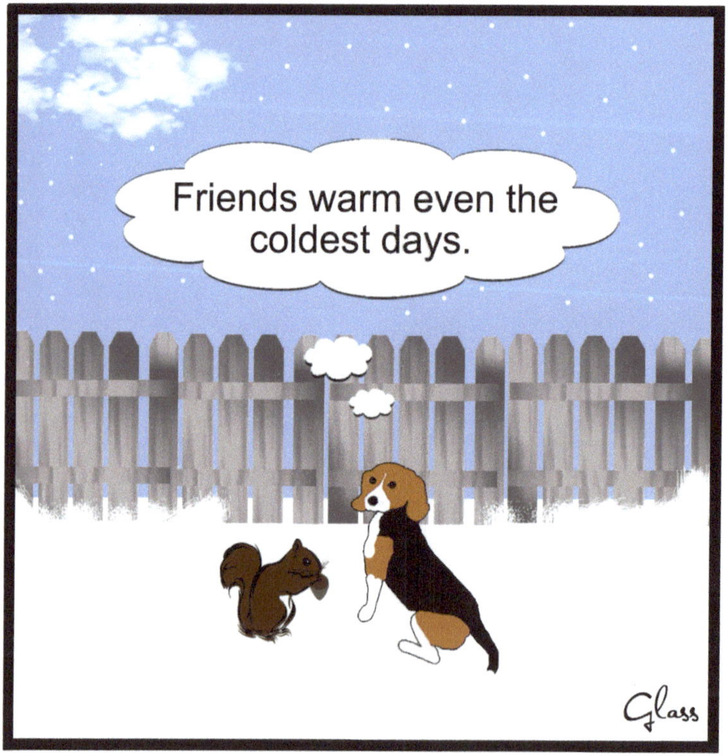
Friends warm even the coldest days.
Glass

Sleepytown Beagles by Timothy Glass

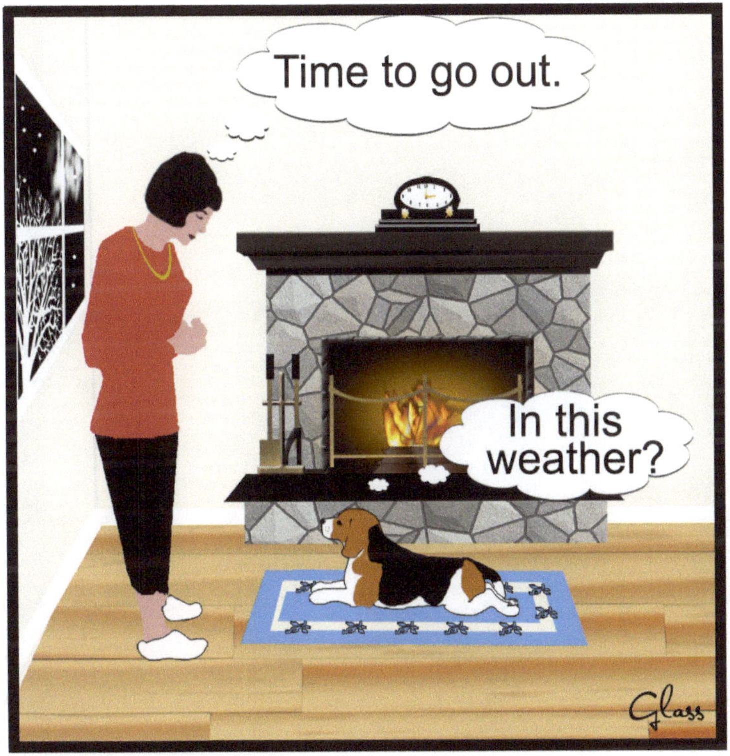
Time to go out.
In this weather?
Glass

Timothy Glass

Sleepytown Beagles by Timothy Glass

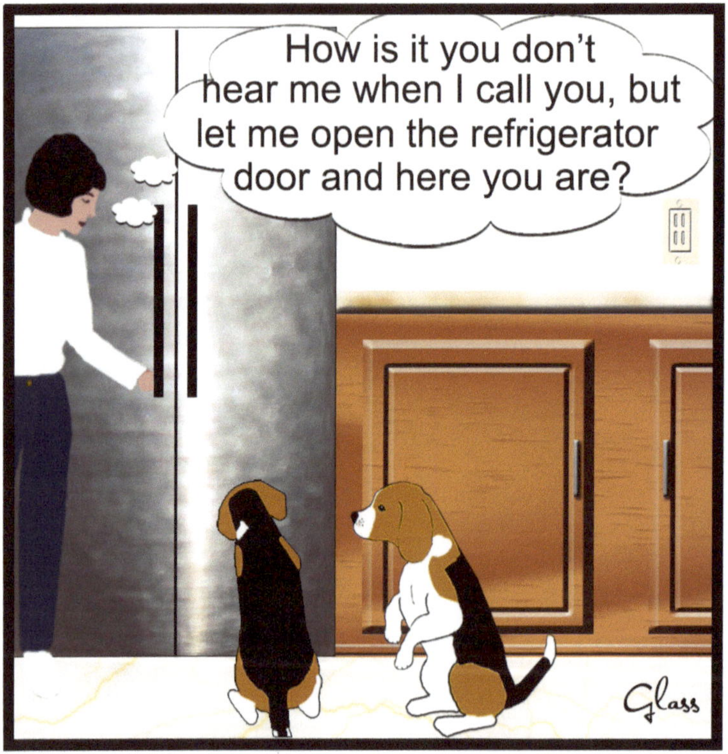
How is it you don't hear me when I call you, but let me open the refrigerator door and here you are?
Glass

Sleepytown Beagles by Timothy Glass

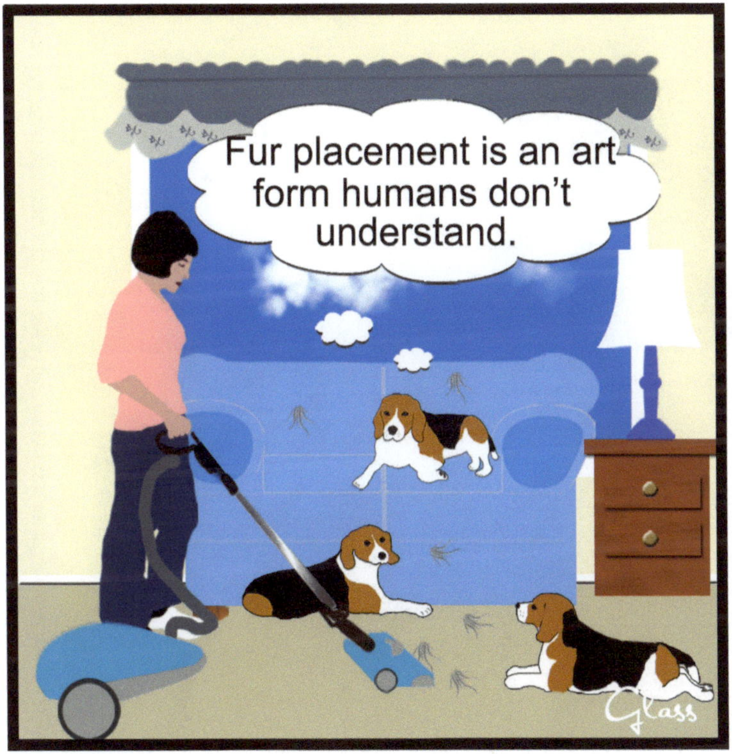
Fur placement is an art form humans don't understand.
Glass

Timothy Glass

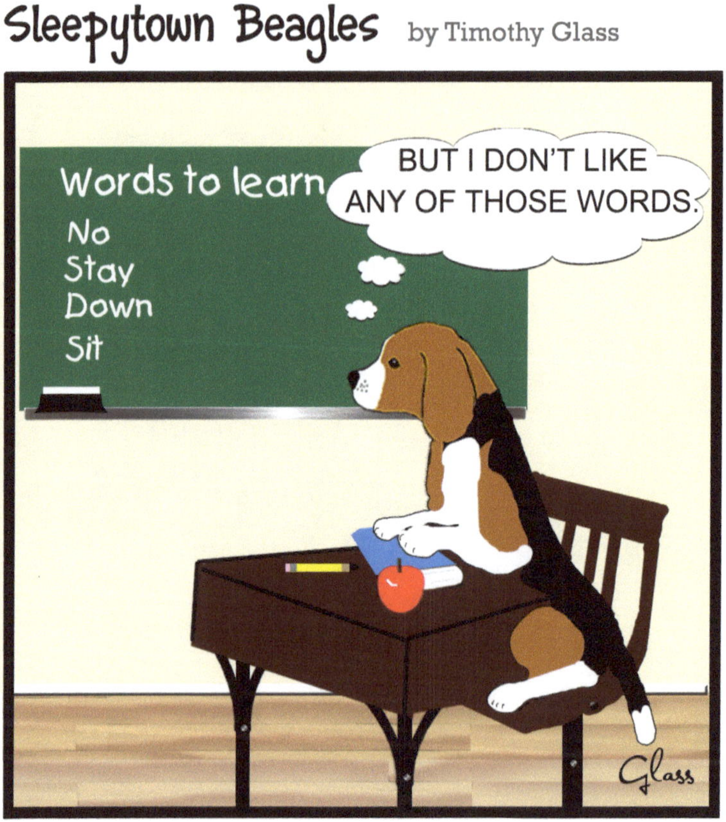
Sleepytown Beagles by Timothy Glass
Words to learn
No
Stay
Down
Sit
BUT I DON'T LIKE ANY OF THOSE WORDS.
Glass

Sleepytown Beagles by Timothy Glass

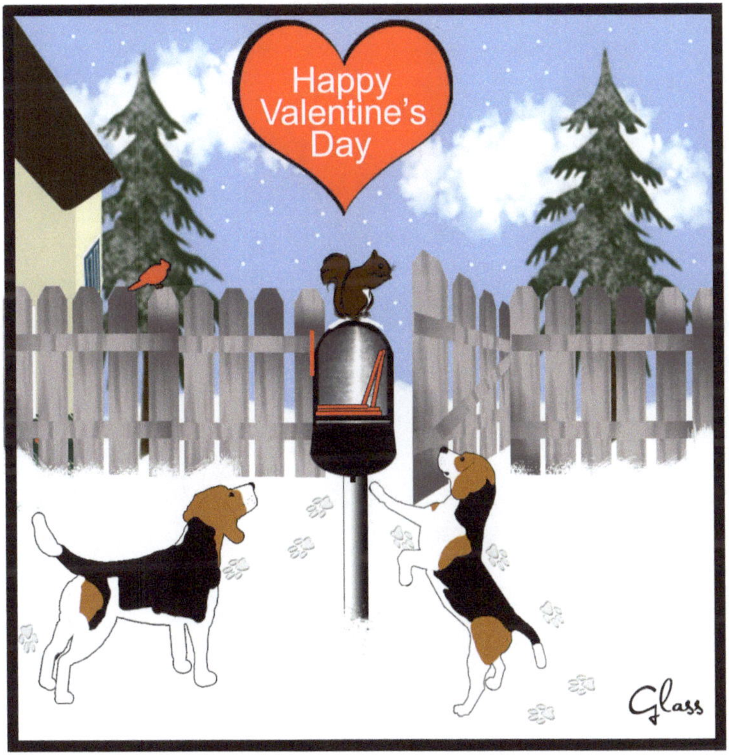
Happy Valentine's Day
Glass

Timothy Glass

Sleepytown Beagles by Timothy Glass

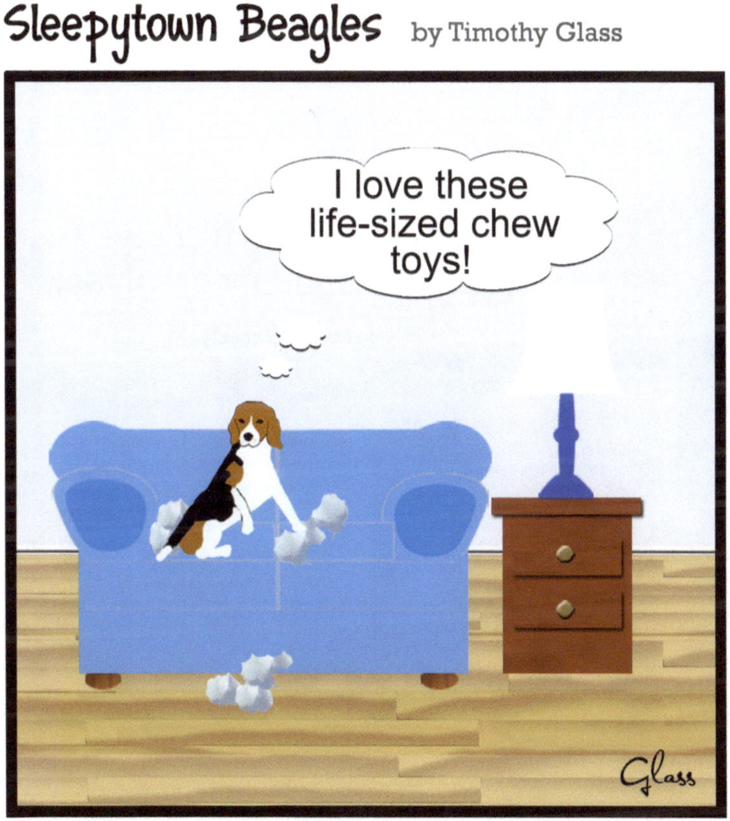
Sleepytown Beagles by Timothy Glass
I love these life-sized chew toys!
Glass

Timothy Glass

Sleepytown Beagles by Timothy Glass

In The Doghouse

Sleepytown Beagles by Timothy Glass

Timothy Glass

Sleepytown Beagles by Timothy Glass

In The Doghouse

Sleepytown Beagles by Timothy Glass

Timothy Glass

Sleepytown Beagles by Timothy Glass

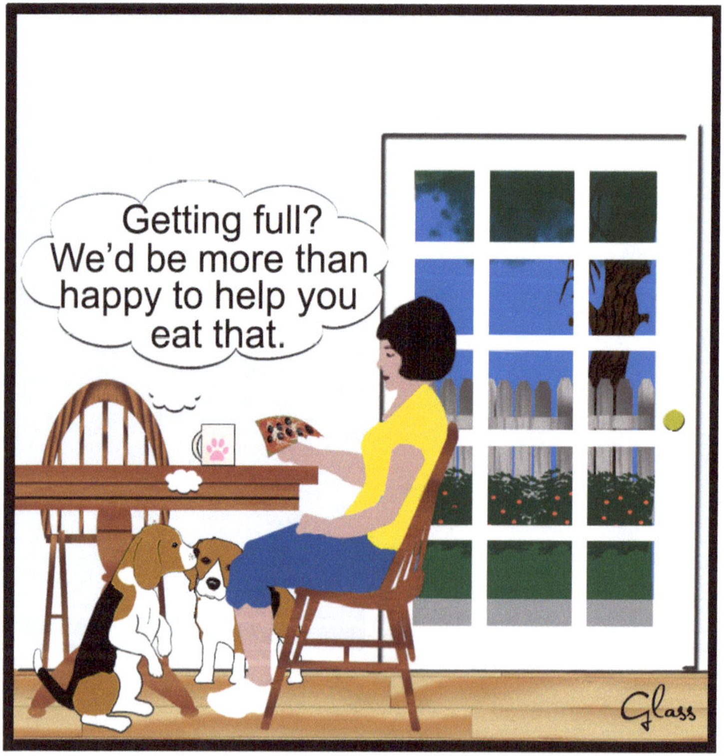
Getting full? We'd be more than happy to help you eat that.
Glass

In The Doghouse

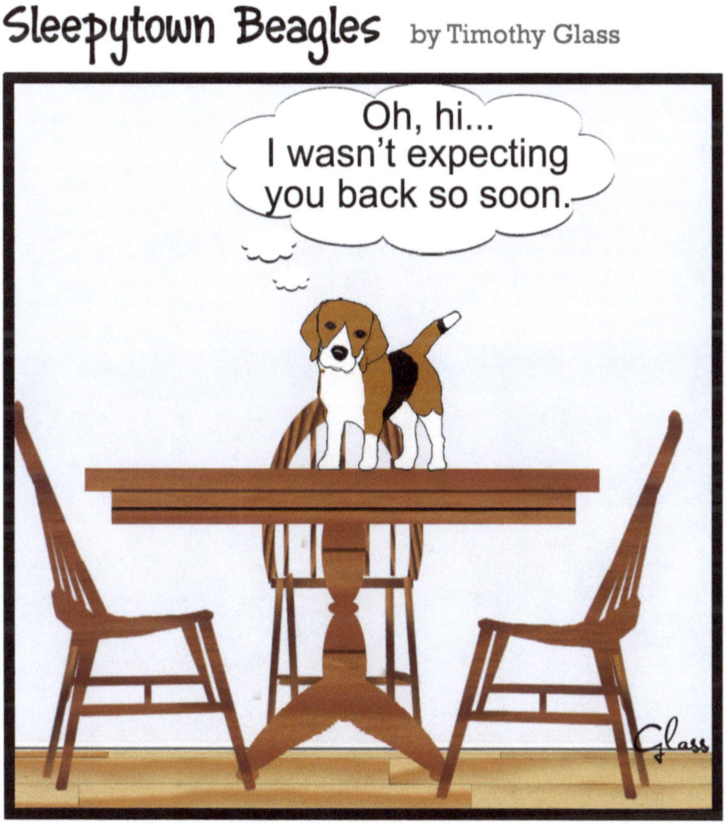
Sleepytown Beagles by Timothy Glass
Oh, hi...
I wasn't expecting
you back so soon.
Glass

Timothy Glass

Sleepytown Beagles by Timothy Glass

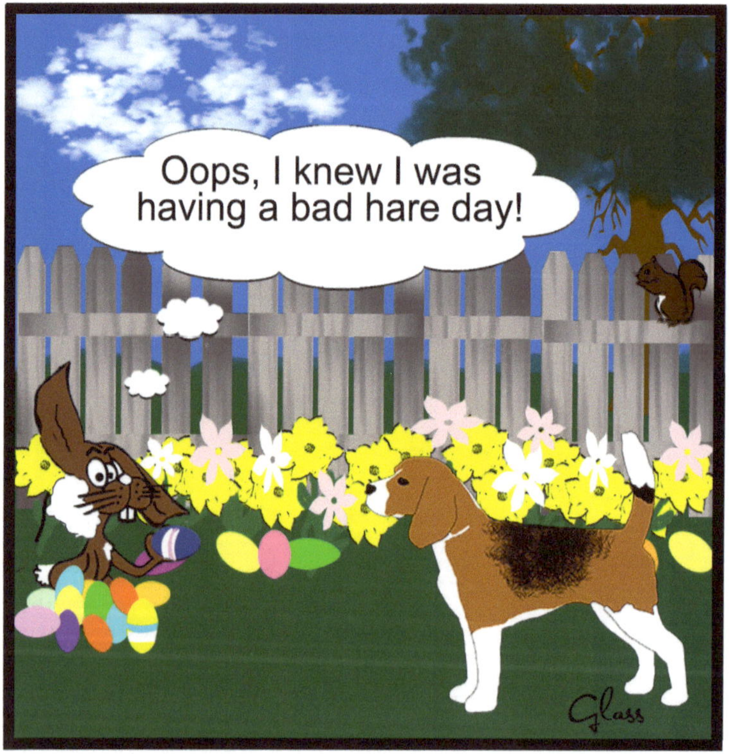
Oops, I knew I was having a bad hare day!
Glass

In The Doghouse

Sleepytown Beagles by Timothy Glass

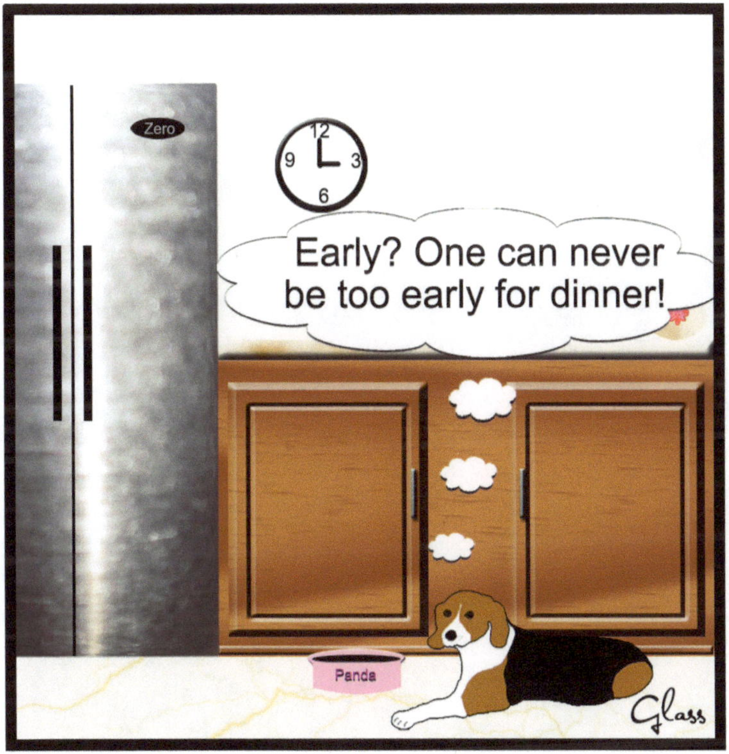
Zero
12
9
3
6
Early? One can never be too early for dinner!
Panda
Glass

Timothy Glass

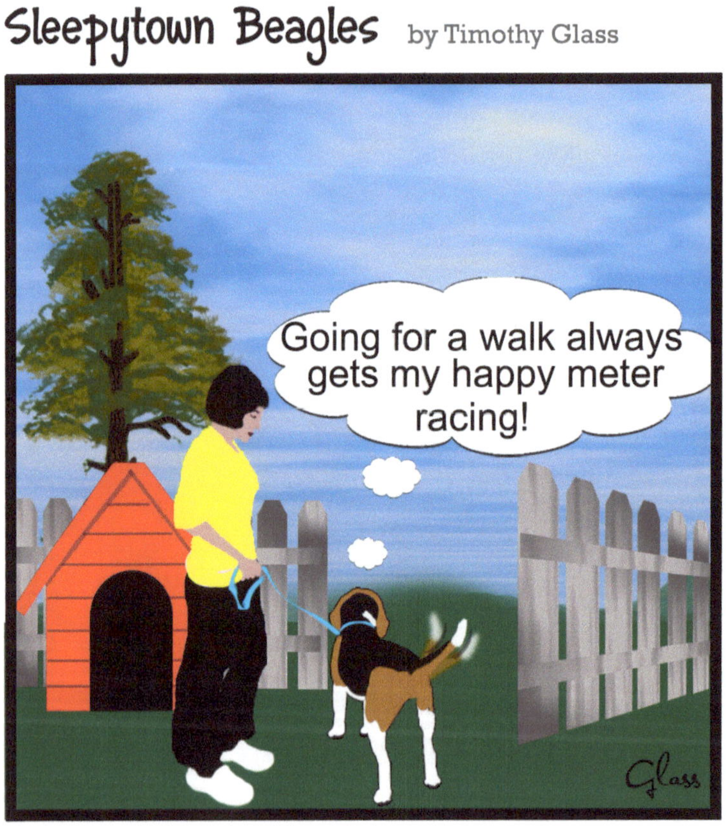
Sleepytown Beagles by Timothy Glass
Going for a walk always gets my happy meter racing!
Glass

In The Doghouse

Sleepytown Beagles by Timothy Glass

Timothy Glass

Sleepytown Beagles   by Timothy Glass

In The Doghouse

Sleepytown Beagles by Timothy Glass

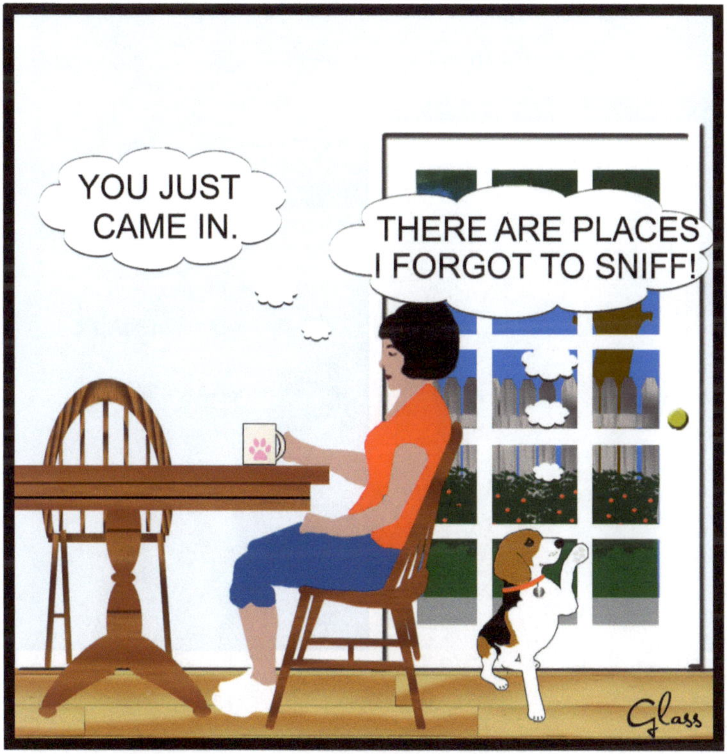
YOU JUST CAME IN.
THERE ARE PLACES I FORGOT TO SNIFF!
Glass

Timothy Glass

Sleepytown Beagles

by Timothy Glass

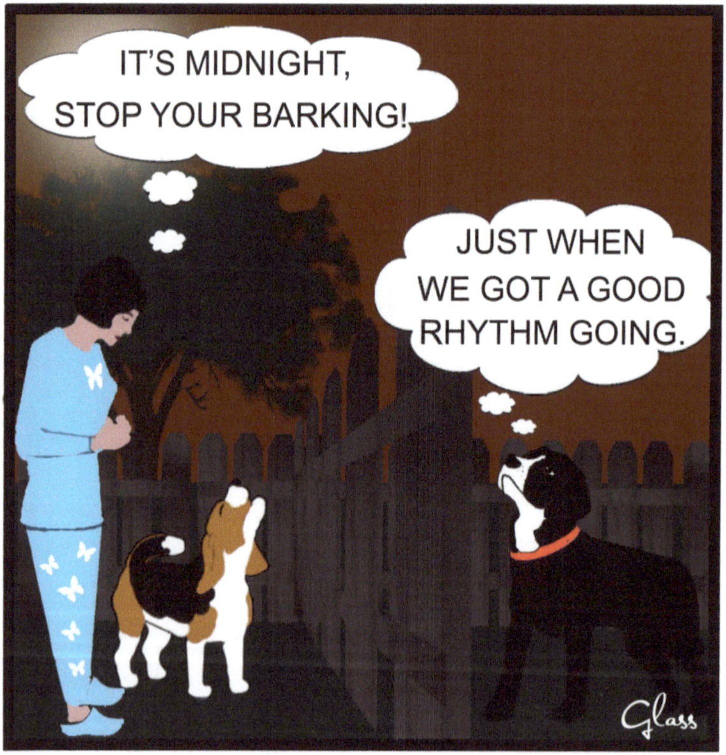
IT'S MIDNIGHT,
STOP YOUR BARKING!
JUST WHEN
WE GOT A GOOD
RHYTHM GOING.
Glass

In The Doghouse

Sleepytown Beagles by Timothy Glass

Timothy Glass

Sleepytown Beagles by Timothy Glass

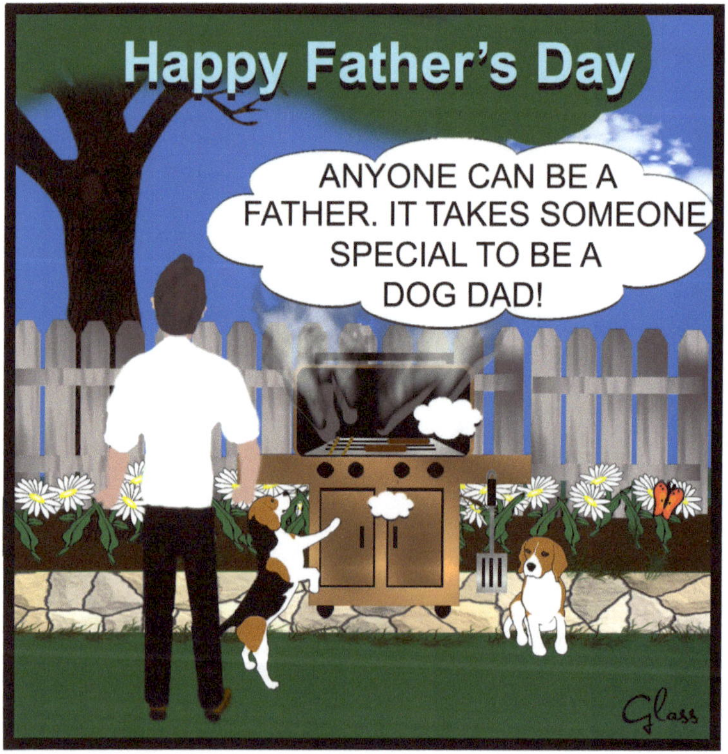
Happy Father's Day
ANYONE CAN BE A FATHER. IT TAKES SOMEONE SPECIAL TO BE A DOG DAD!
Glass

Sleepytown Beagles by Timothy Glass

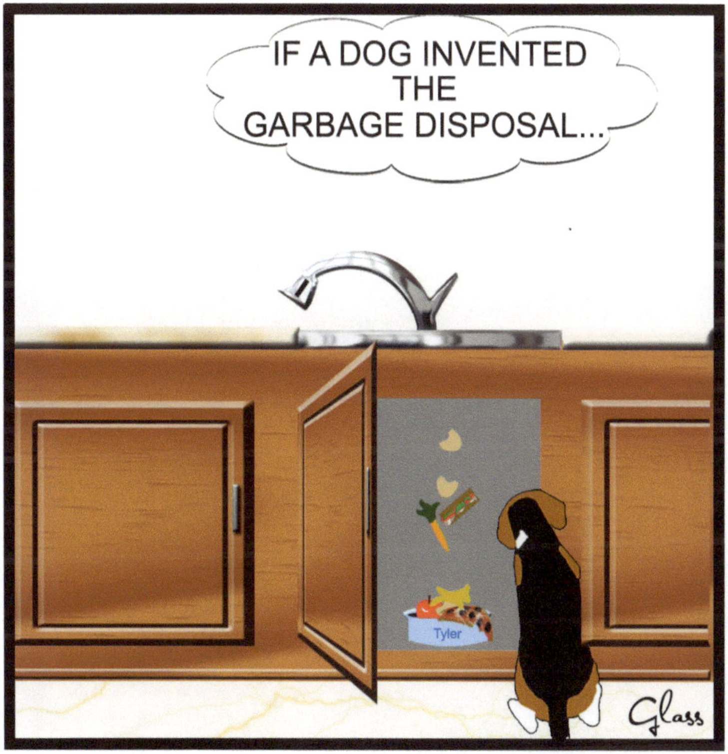
IF A DOG INVENTED THE GARBAGE DISPOSAL...
Tyler
Glass

Timothy Glass

Sleepytown Beagles by Timothy Glass

In The Doghouse

Sleepytown Beagles by Timothy Glass

Timothy Glass

Sleepytown Beagles by Timothy Glass

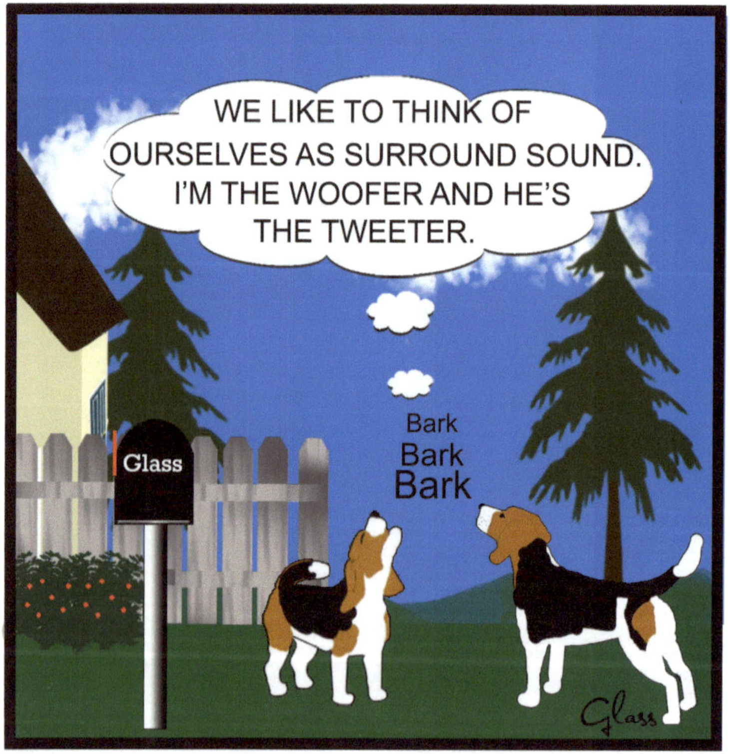
WE LIKE TO THINK OF OURSELVES AS SURROUND SOUND. I'M THE WOOFER AND HE'S THE TWEETER.
Bark
Bark
Bark
Glass
Glass

In The Doghouse

Sleepytown Beagles by Timothy Glass

Timothy Glass

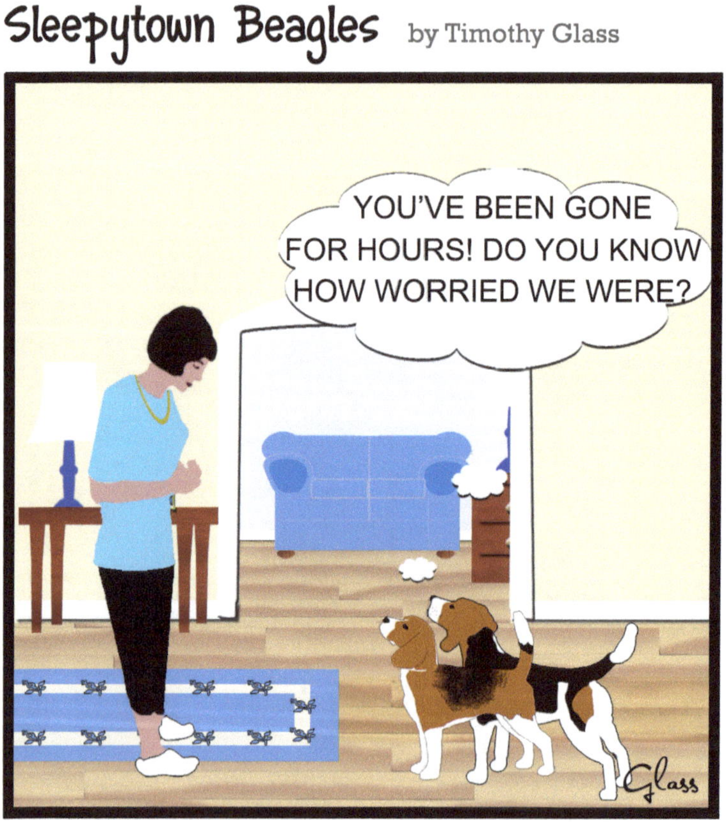
Sleepytown Beagles by Timothy Glass
YOU'VE BEEN GONE FOR HOURS! DO YOU KNOW HOW WORRIED WE WERE?
Glass

In The Doghouse

Sleepytown Beagles by Timothy Glass

Timothy Glass

Sleepytown Beagles by Timothy Glass

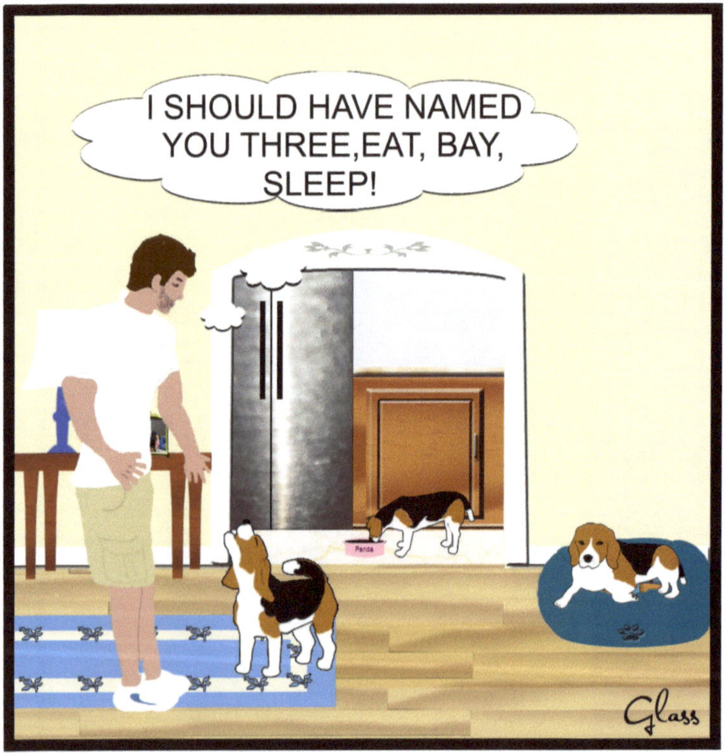
I SHOULD HAVE NAMED YOU THREE,EAT, BAY, SLEEP!
Glass

In The Doghouse

Sleepytown Beagles by Timothy Glass

Timothy Glass

Sleepytown Beagles by Timothy Glass

In The Doghouse

Sleepytown Beagles by Timothy Glass

Timothy Glass

Sleepytown Beagles by Timothy Glass

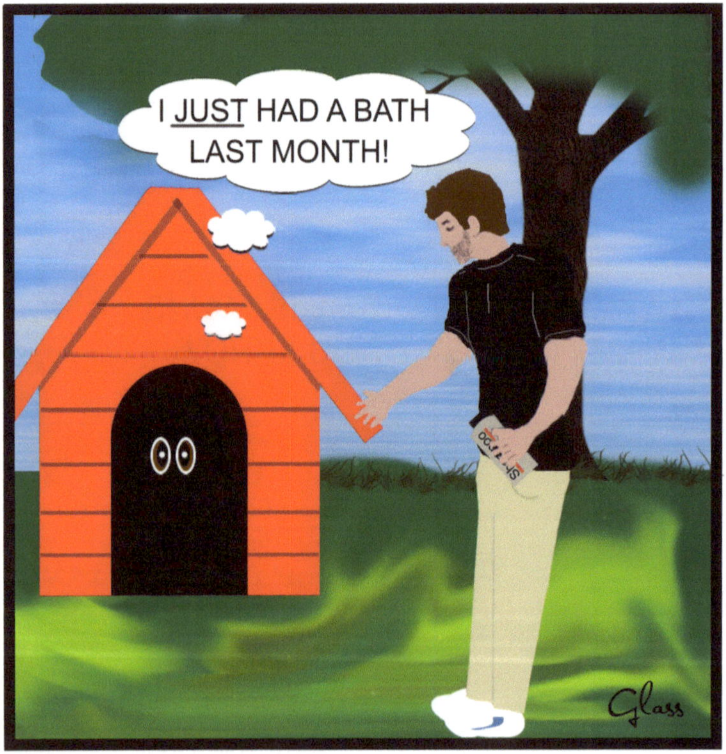
I JUST HAD A BATH LAST MONTH!
Glass

In The Doghouse

Sleepytown Beagles by Timothy Glass

Sleepytown Beagles by Timothy Glass

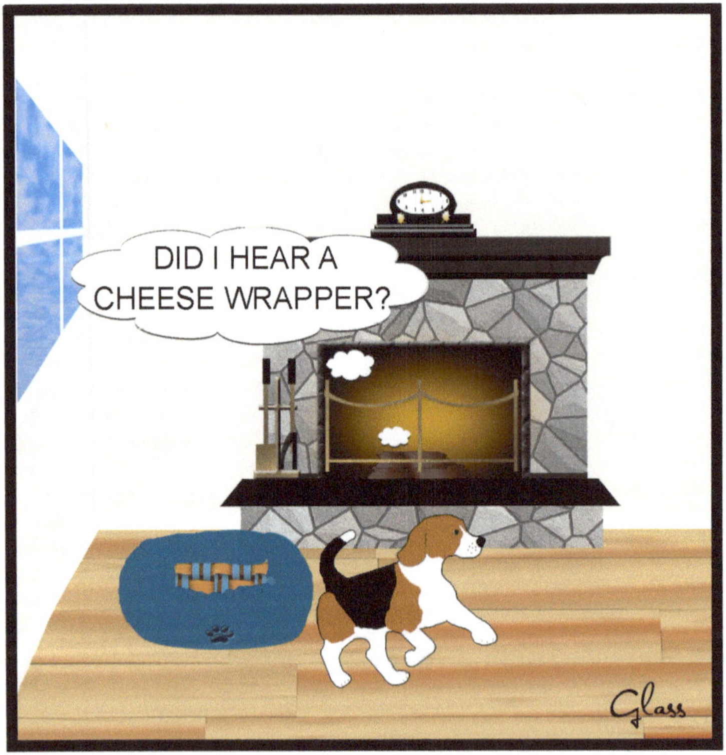
DID I HEAR A
CHEESE WRAPPER?
Glass

Sleepytown Beagles by Timothy Glass

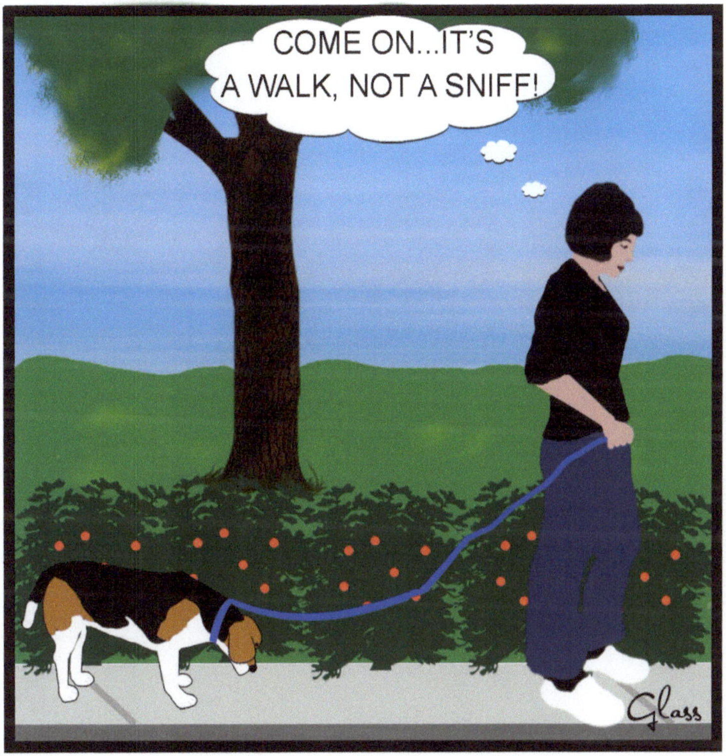
COME ON...IT'S A WALK, NOT A SNIFF!
Glass

Timothy Glass

Sleepytown Beagles by Timothy Glass

In The Doghouse

Sleepytown Beagles by Timothy Glass

Timothy Glass

Sleepytown Beagles by Timothy Glass

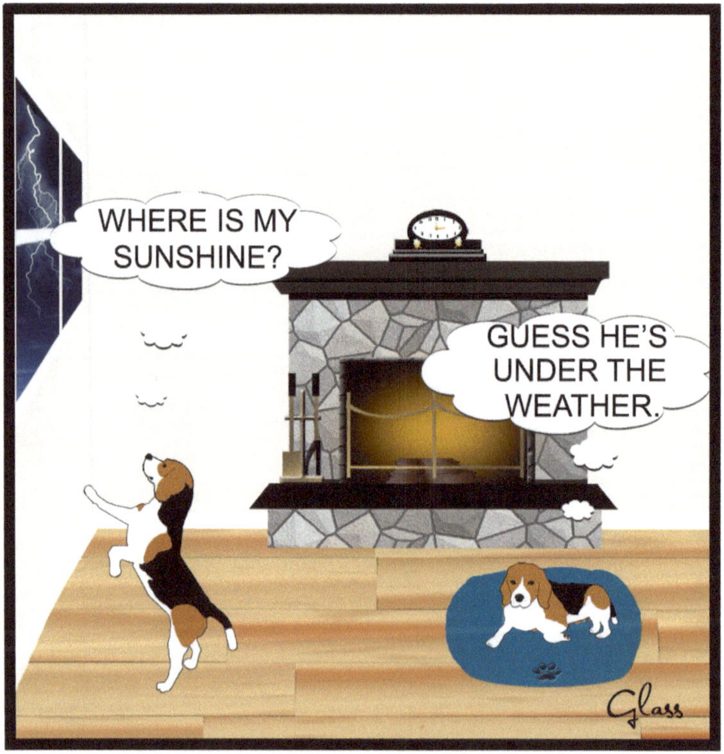
WHERE IS MY SUNSHINE?
GUESS HE'S UNDER THE WEATHER.
Glass

In The Doghouse

Sleepytown Beagles by Timothy Glass

Timothy Glass

Sleepytown Beagles by Timothy Glass

Sleepytown Beagles by Timothy Glass

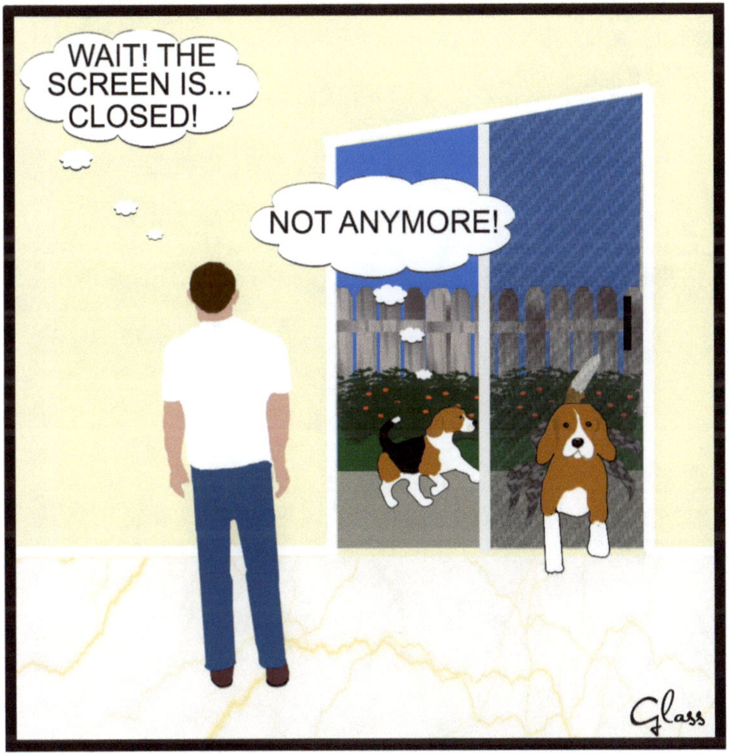
WAIT! THE SCREEN IS... CLOSED!
NOT ANYMORE!
Glass

Sleepytown Beagles by Timothy Glass

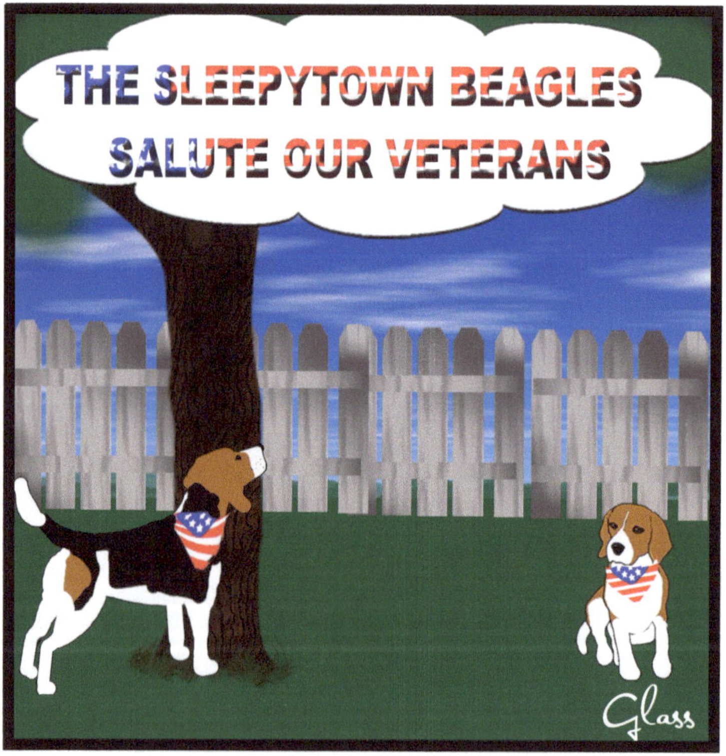
THE SLEEPYTOWN BEAGLES
SALUTE OUR VETERANS
Glass

Sleepytown Beagles by Timothy Glass

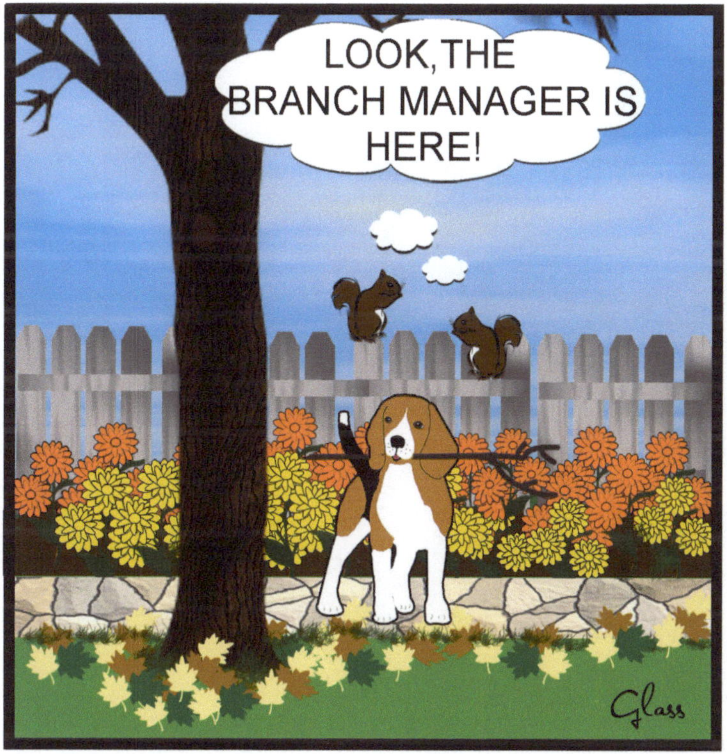
LOOK, THE BRANCH MANAGER IS HERE!
Glass

Timothy Glass

Sleepytown Beagles by Timothy Glass

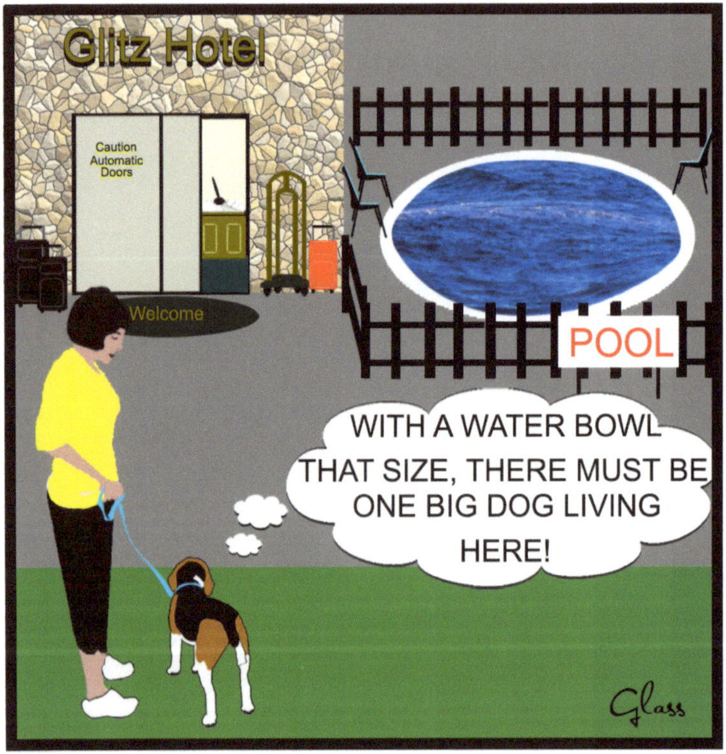
Glitz Hotel
Caution Automatic Doors
Welcome
POOL
WITH A WATER BOWL THAT SIZE, THERE MUST BE ONE BIG DOG LIVING HERE!
Glass

In The Doghouse

Sleepytown Beagles by Timothy Glass

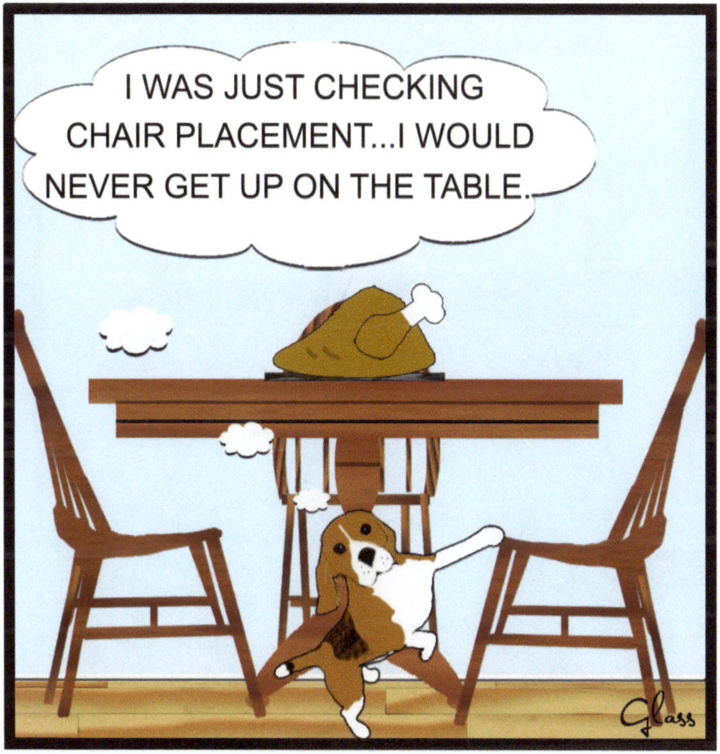
I WAS JUST CHECKING CHAIR PLACEMENT...I WOULD NEVER GET UP ON THE TABLE.
Glass

Timothy Glass

Sleepytown Beagles by Timothy Glass

In The Doghouse

Sleepytown Beagles by Timothy Glass

Timothy Glass

Sleepytown Beagles by Timothy Glass

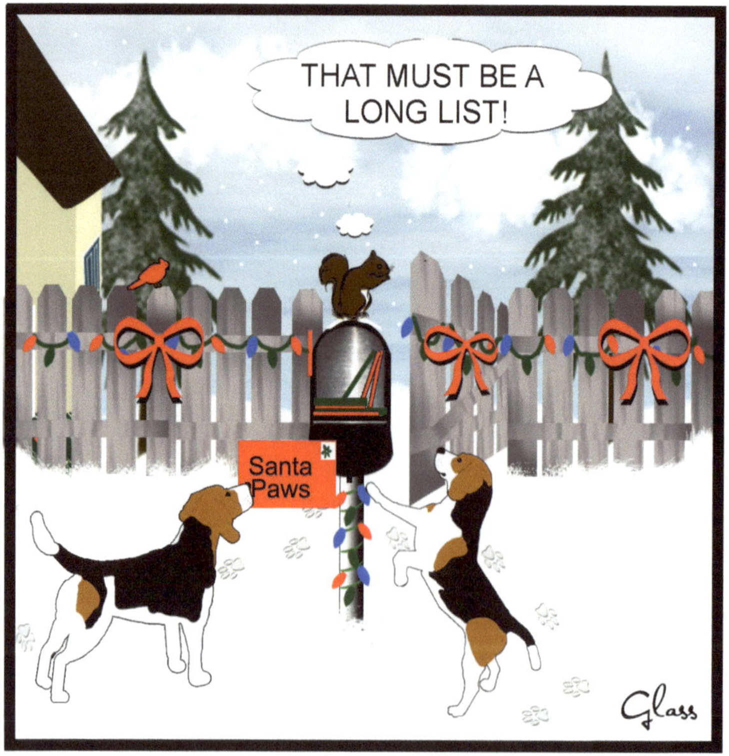
THAT MUST BE A LONG LIST!
Santa Paws
Glass

In The Doghouse

Sleepytown Beagles by Timothy Glass

Timothy Glass

Sleepytown Beagles by Timothy Glass

In The Doghouse

Sleepytown Beagles by Timothy Glass

Timothy Glass

Sleepytown Beagles by Timothy Glass

In The Doghouse

Sleepytown Beagles by Timothy Glass

Timothy Glass

Sleepytown Beagles by Timothy Glass

In The Doghouse

Sleepytown Beagles by Timothy Glass

Timothy Glass

Sleepytown Beagles by Timothy Glass

In The Doghouse

Sleepytown Beagles by Timothy Glass

Timothy Glass

Sleepytown Beagles by Timothy Glass

In The Doghouse

Sleepytown Beagles by Timothy Glass

Timothy Glass

Sleepytown Beagles by Timothy Glass

In The Doghouse

Sleepytown Beagles by Timothy Glass

Timothy Glass

Sleepytown Beagles by Timothy Glass

In The Doghouse

Sleepytown Beagles by Timothy Glass

Timothy Glass

Sleepytown Beagles by Timothy Glass

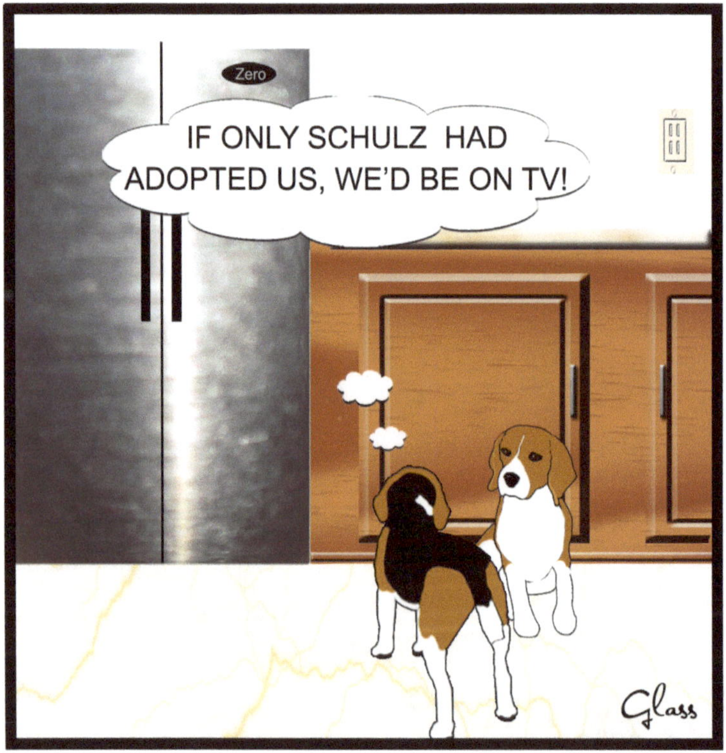

Zero
IF ONLY SCHULZ HAD ADOPTED US, WE'D BE ON TV!
Glass

Sleepytown Beagles by Timothy Glass

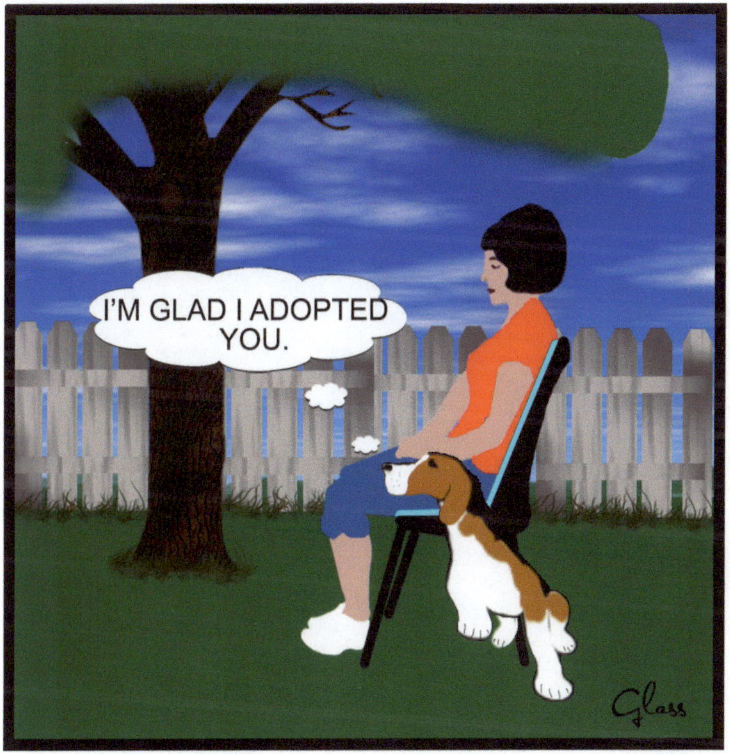
I'M GLAD I ADOPTED YOU.
Glass

Timothy Glass

Sleepytown Beagles by Timothy Glass

In The Doghouse

Sleepytown Beagles by Timothy Glass

Timothy Glass

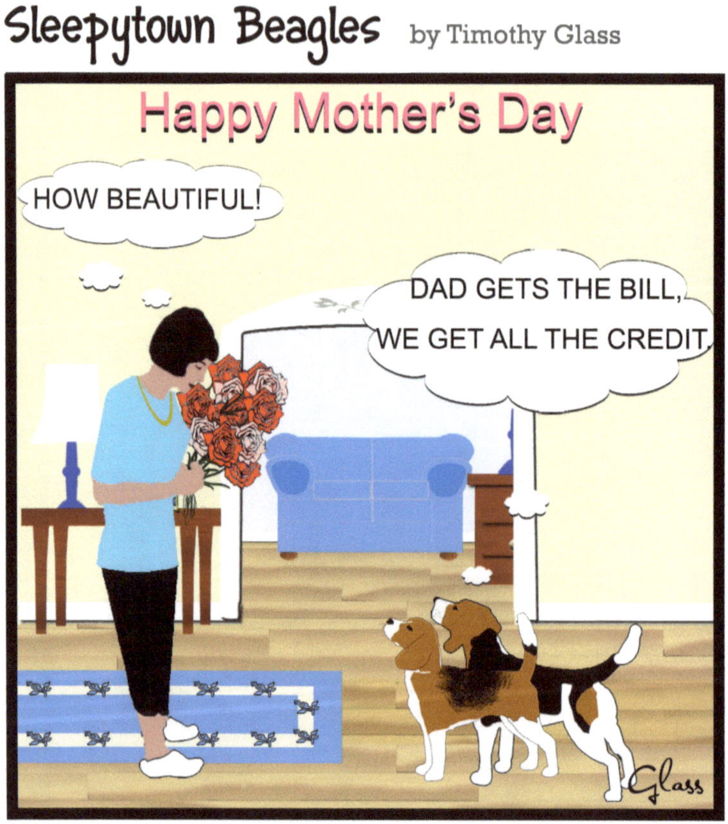
Sleepytown Beagles by Timothy Glass
Happy Mother's Day
HOW BEAUTIFUL!
DAD GETS THE BILL,
WE GET ALL THE CREDIT.
Glass

In The Doghouse

Sleepytown Beagles by Timothy Glass

Timothy Glass

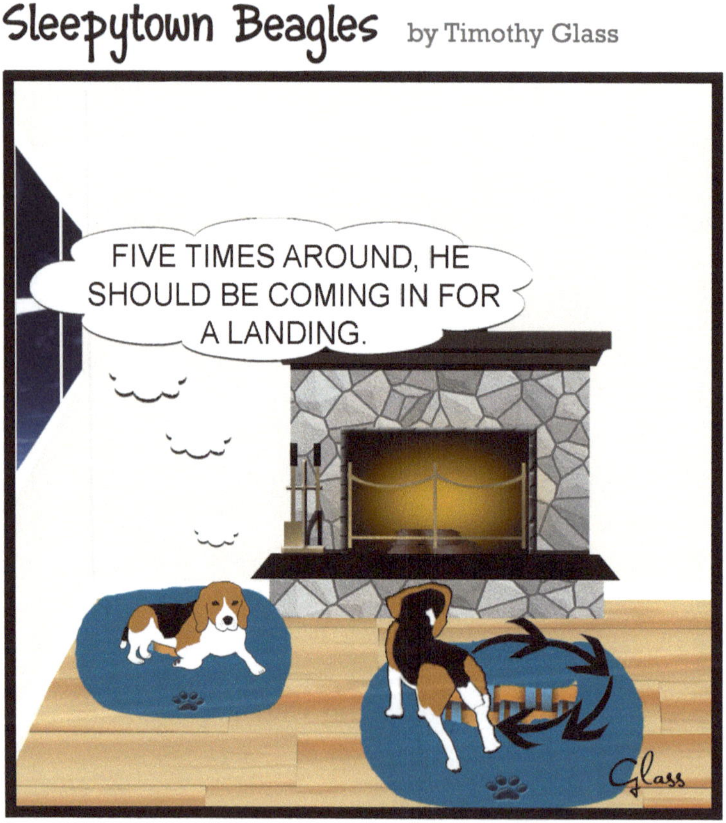
Sleepytown Beagles by Timothy Glass
FIVE TIMES AROUND, HE SHOULD BE COMING IN FOR A LANDING.
Glass

Sleepytown Beagles by Timothy Glass

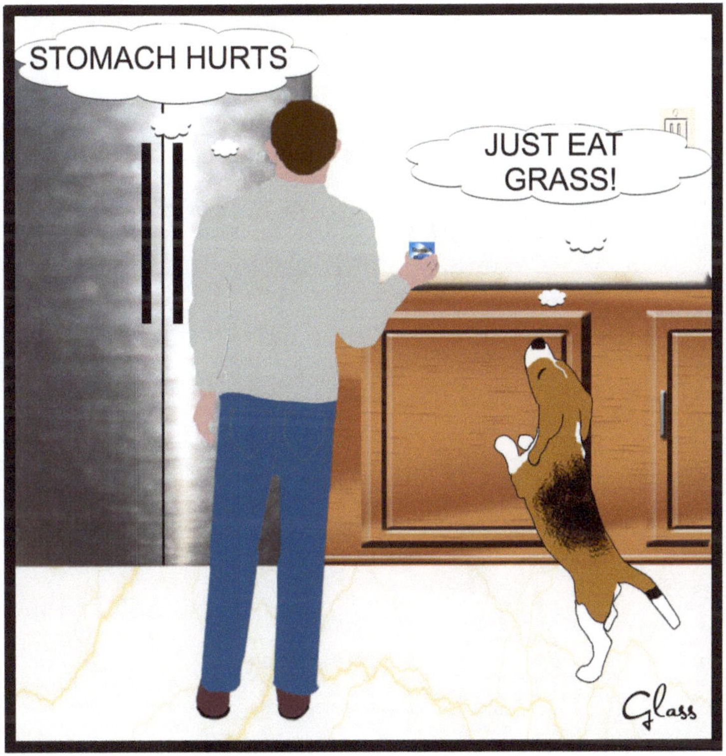
STOMACH HURTS
JUST EAT GRASS!
Glass

Timothy Glass

Sleepytown Beagles by Timothy Glass

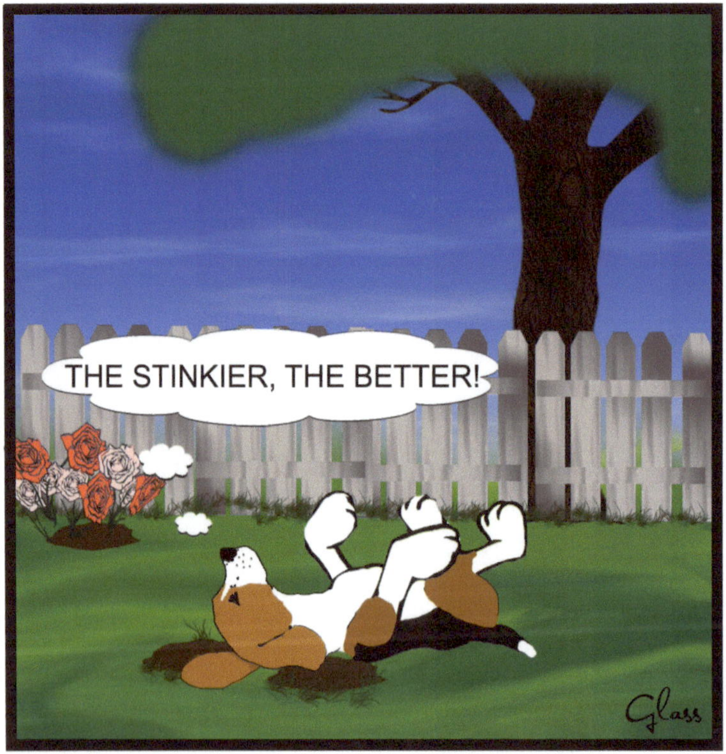
THE STINKIER, THE BETTER!
Glass

Sleepytown Beagles by Timothy Glass

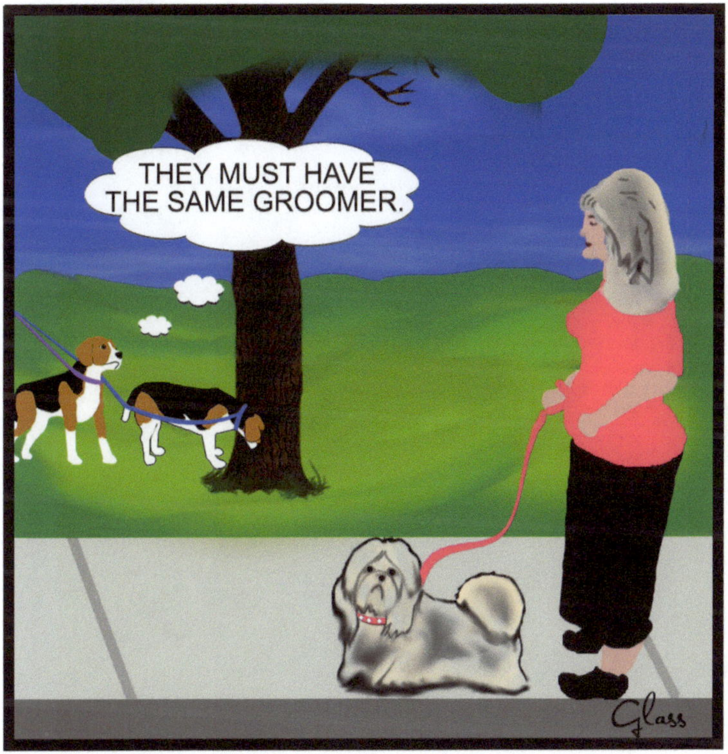
THEY MUST HAVE
THE SAME GROOMER.
Glass

Timothy Glass

Sleepytown Beagles by Timothy Glass

In The Doghouse

Sleepytown Beagles by Timothy Glass

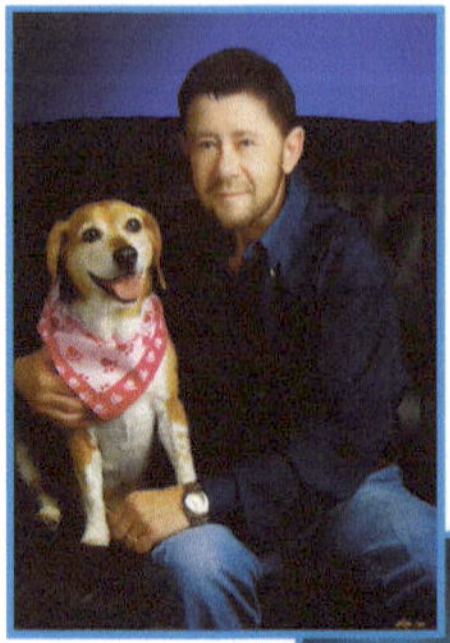

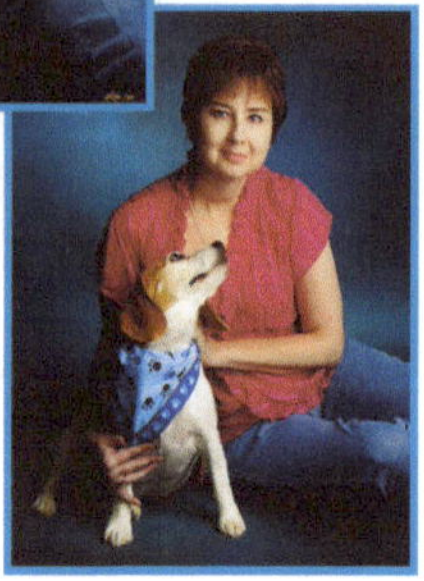

It was always my dream to be a cartoonist. The commercial art school I attended in Westport, Connecticut offered classes in this medium, and I was hooked. I was on the dean's list under the school's founder, Norman Rockwell. While my mother and father always believed I was gifted in art, I ultimately put aside my dream and studied Computer Science at the University of New Mexico. It wasn't until 1998, when I was almost killed in a tragic accident with a drunk driver, that I began to put pen to pad. I illustrated my children's books and then a burning desire to create my own cartoon feature emerged once more. In 2010 the Sleepytown Beagles cartoons began to spread around the world, becoming a regular and requested feature in a magazine in the UK. In 2012 the cartoons became a regular feature on GoComics.

The truth of the matter is, our beagles run the show in the Glass household. They always supply me with fresh material. Our love for the beagles goes beyond words. For this reason, I chose to draw the cartoons from a dog's perspective on life.

I hope you have enjoyed this first book, and there are more to follow. Book reviews are crucial, both for me as the author and for your fellow readers. Please take the time to leave a review at your favorite bookseller. I would greatly appreciate it.

Other Books By Timothy Glass

Children's Books

Sleepytown Beagles, Panda Meets Ms. Daisy Bloom
Sleepytown Beagles, Penny's 4th of July
Sleepytown Beagles, Oh Brother
Sleepytown Beagles, Differences
Sleepytown Beagles, The Lemonade Stand
Sleepytown Beagles, Jingle Beagles
Sleepytown Beagles, Up, Up and Away

Nonfiction Books

Just This Side of Heaven

Fiction

Postcards
Sleepytown Beagles, Doggone It

Visit Tim's website at **www.timglass.com** Also, don't forget to check out his beagle cartoons at http://www.timglass.com/Cartoons/

Join Tim on his fan pages:

Facebook: https://www.facebook.com/pages/Timothy-Glass/146746625258?ref=ts

Twitter: www.twitter.com/timothyglass/

LinkedIn: http://www.linkedin.com/in/timothyglass

Check out our Sleepytown Beagles fabric and wrapping paper

https://www.spoonflower.com/profiles/sleepytown_beagles

Watch for our next book, coming soon!

www.ingramcontent.com/pod-product-compliance
Lightning Source LLC
Chambersburg PA
CBHW042008150426
43195CB00002B/57